Power and Elusiveness in Shelley

OSCAR W. FIRKINS

1970
OCTAGON BOOKS
New York

Copyright 1937 by the University of Minnesota
Copyright renewed 1965 by the University of Minnesota

Reprinted 1970
by special arrangement with the University of Minnesota Press

OCTAGON BOOKS
A DIVISION OF FARRAR, STRAUS & GIROUX, INC.
19 Union Square West
New York, N. Y. 10003

LIBRARY OF CONGRESS CATALOG CARD NUMBER: 70-120253

PR
5438
.F5
1970

CONTENTS

INTRODUCTION	3
ABSTRACTION	4
SPACE	12
TIME	16
THE MIND: THE PASSIONS	30
PRESENTATION OF MIND IN TERMS OF MATTER	32
PRESENTATION OF MATTER IN TERMS OF MIND	47
MIXTURE OF MATTER AND SPIRIT	56
SLEEP	66
DREAMS	73
UNEARTHLY BEINGS	81
LANDSCAPE	89
WIND	92
CLOUD	100
LIGHT	110
SOUND	118
ODOR	126
COORDINATION	131
ASSIMILATION	136

Penetration and Absorption	145
Effluence	156
Pantheism	171
Metaphysics	181
Summary	185

POWER AND ELUSIVENESS
IN SHELLEY

Introduction

EVERYONE knows that Shelley loved the abstract, that the ideas in his mind were wont to present themselves as qualities and forces. An appreciation of Shelley may almost be said to start from the perception of this fact.

I believe that this love of abstraction is only one form — probably the most obvious and the most significant form — of a larger and more general tendency, or, if the phrase be preferred, that it is the chief member in a group of tendencies.

The object of this essay is to collect and combine the manifestations of this larger tendency.

The abstract ideas which Shelley loved are characterized by width and weight of import united with a want of precision and distinction in their content. I believe that ideas of this kind — ideas which combine momentousness of import with indistinctness of material — appealed in a great variety of forms to the sympathy and interest of Shelley.

The truth as thus stated has no claim to novelty or value: most critics would probably admit its validity at the start. The value of this essay, should it prove to possess any value, will be found in the nature and variety of the illustrations I shall endeavor to furnish.

I proceed without further preface to the detail of these illustrations. The Forman Edition (1880) of Shelley's works has been used.

Abstraction

THE LOVE of abstraction dominated the work of Shelley at every period of his literary life. His earliest well-known poem, *Queen Mab,* begins:

> How wonderful is Death,
> Death and his brother Sleep! [1]

The poem which he left unfinished at the time of his death, *The Triumph of Life,* is abstract even to the wording of its title.

Abstraction may appear in early youth as the makeshift of inexperience, the attempt to supply or to disguise the poverty of the unripe imagination. It may appear in later life in combination with the intellectual and rational powers which mark the maturing of the thought and the subsidence of the imaginative energy. The remarkable thing about the abstraction of Shelley is that it is not associated with any poverty of imagination, and that—in his poetry—it is unaccompanied by any high development of the logical and intellectual capacities.

I speak of his poetry in the last instance because no one can read the letters, notes, and prefaces, to say nothing of the essays, of Shelley, without feeling that the limitation applies rather to his poetry than to his mind. It remains true and remarkable that poetry showing the imagination at its noontide and the intel-

[1] *Queen Mab,* i. 1–2.

lect at its dawn should have been penetrated and controlled by this element of abstraction.

The element shows itself both in the substantial framework of the poems and in the texture of the style.

Queen Mab is, as it were, an epic of humanity, and the fairy herself typifies the cosmic imagination.

Alastor bears as its second or alternate title "The Spirit of Solitude."

In *Prometheus Unbound* Prometheus represents Humanity, and Asia, Nature; the Earth and the Moon, to omit minor figures, are introduced as personalities chanting in maenadic exultation.

The Mask of Anarchy confesses its abstraction in its title.

The Witch of Atlas embodies, in Professor Dowden's words, "the great and beneficent enchantress — she whose shadow is the beauty of the world." [2]

Epipsychidion is an incarnation of the spirit of love and beauty in a human shape.

The Triumph of Life is an allegory of individual and racial destiny.

It is, moreover, to be observed that among Shelley's prose works the most notorious, *The Necessity of Atheism,* and the most illustrious, *A Defence of Poetry,* are devoted, as their very titles show, to the elucidation of abstractions.

Furthermore, the poems which are theoretically concrete, such as *Hellas* and *Adonais,* are all but as abstract

[2] Edward Dowden, *Life of Shelley* (2 vols., London, 1886), II, 340.

as their companions, and the characters which are nominally individual, Laon, Cythna, Lionel, and Mahmud, are only less representative than the confessed abstractions. Emilia Viviani and John Keats, both of whom were acquaintances of Shelley, become the subjects of poems as abstract and ethereal in texture as the dreams and whimsies of a less idealistic poet.

It was inevitable that a mind of this stamp should take the last step in the path of generalization, that it should find repose and delight in the contemplation of the ultimate principle and groundwork of the universe. This step is taken in the *Hymn to Intellectual Beauty,* in *Mont Blanc,* in the *Lines written among the Euganean Hills,*[3] in *Queen Mab,*[4] in *Alastor,*[5] in *Adonais,*[6] and in *The Sensitive Plant;* in which last the Lady apparently typifies the power whose presence vitalizes and blesses the universe and whose withdrawal would expose all its subjects and creatures to the inroads of disease and decay.

Such is the evidence offered by the structure of the poems. The testimony of style is also of value. The occurrence of abstract nouns, usually capitalized to indicate the wish to personify, is one of the most omnipresent and noticeable features of Shelley's poetry. These may be:

A. Names of virtues or the like: Love, Gentleness, Mercy, Pity, Peace, Patience, Courage of soul,[7] elevated will, Conscience, Virtue, justice, Liberty.

---

[3] Lines 294-319.   [4] vi. 146-238.   [5] Lines 1-49.   [6] Stanzas liv-lv.
[7] I follow Shelley in the use or non-use of capitals.

B. Names of evils or scourges: Fear, "spectral Terror," Panic, Dread the murderer, Revenge, Vengeance, Hate, Enmity, Pride, Avarice, Selfishness, Wrong, Fraud, Calumny, Falsehood, Hypocrisy, Shame, Despair, Sin, Guilt, Murder, Care, Infirmity, Sorrow, Melancholy, Woe, Disquiet, Discord, Strife, War, Defeat, Danger, Rapine, Slaughter, Carnage, Destruction, Ruin, Desolation, Death, Blight, Decay, Plague, Pestilence, Poison, Earthquake, Famine, Want, Toil, Anarchy, Oppression, Tyranny, Dominion, Misrule, Empire, Conspiracy, Slavery, Folly, Error, Custom, Madness, Religion, Faith, The Grave, Hell.

C. Names of kindly or beneficent abstractions, not distinctly ethical: Verse, Art, Fame, Philosophy, Truth, Reason, Wisdom, Silence, Solitude, Security, Expectation, Hope, Pleasure, Joy, Victory, Equality, Loveliness.

D. Time and its divisions: Time, The Past, the Present, the Future, Eternity, Spring, Summer, Autumn, Winter, April, Morning, Twilight, Youth. Spatial abstractions: the Earth, the Moon.

E. Intangible abstractions: Life, Birth, Destiny, Necessity.

Love and Freedom would perhaps hold the places of eminence in this list. The most remarkable feature in the catalogue, which, though not exhaustive, is trustworthy in the view it suggests of Shelley's habits, is the fullness of the list of evils and scourges in contrast with the meagerness of the group of virtues. If we leave out love, justice, and possibly pity, the specific virtues are not copiously personified in Shelley, while his imagination revels in the multiplication of that kind of abstraction with which evil and suffering are inseparably connected. It cannot be said that he dwells at more length or with more fervor on the pests which he detests and deplores than on the fewer virtues which he selects for laudation: but his mind, in the contemplation of goodness, was impelled to concentrate and amplify, while in the portrayal of evil it expanded and diversified.

Another point in Shelley's treatment of abstractions is his habit of disposing them in groups:

Faith and Plague and Slaughter;[8] Fear and Disquiet and Strife;[9] Madness and Fear and Plague and Famine;[10] virtue, love, and pleasure;[11] Nature, or God, or Love, or Pleasure or Sympathy;[12] Scorn and Hate, Revenge and Selfishness are desolate;[13] Earthquake, Plague and Want;[14] Faith and Folly, Custom and Hell and Mortal Melancholy,[15] upon whose ripe gray hairs Sit Care and Sorrow and Infirmity;[16] With love and life and light and deity;[17]

> Lo! Plague is free
> To Waste, Blight, Poison, Earthquake, Hail and Snow,
> Disease and Want and worse Necessity
> Of hate and ill, and Pride, and Fear, and Tyranny![18]

---

[8] *The Revolt of Islam*, X. xvii. 8.   [9] *Ibid.*, X. xxiii. 1.
[10] *Ibid.*, X. xliv. 2.   [11] *Queen Mab*, ix. 75.
[12] *The Revolt of Islam*, V. li. st. 2. ll. 9–10.
[13] *Ibid.*, V. li. st. 2. ll. 12–13.   [14] *Ibid.*, IX. xiii. 9.
[15] *Ibid.*, V. li. st. 1. ll. 4–5.   [16] *Hellas*, 904–06.
[17] *Epipsychidion*, 112–13.   [18] *The Revolt of Islam*, VIII. v. 6–9.

ABSTRACTION

He is fond of linking the passions by filial or fraternal bonds—a habit which may have been induced or suggested by the genealogies in the *Symposium* of his loved Plato or those which adorn the *Comus* and the *L'Allegro* and *Il Penseroso* of Milton,

And Enmity is sister unto Shame [19]

And Hate is throned on high with Fear his mother [20]

       for Hope and Youth
Are children of one mother, even Love [21]

         Hope is strong,
Justice and Truth their wingèd child have found [22]

        as the star of Death
And Birth is worshipped by those sisters wild
Called Hope and Fear [23]

       Ruin calls
His brother Death.[24]

Son and Mother, Sin and Death [25]

Silence and Twilight, here, twin-sisters, keep
Their noonday watch [26]

Twin-sister of religion, selfishness! [27]

Revenge and Wrong bring forth their kind,
The foul cubs like their parents are [28]

Famine, than whom Misrule no deadlier daughter
Feeds from her thousand breasts, though sleeping there
With lidless eyes lie Faith and Plague and Slaughter,[29]

[19] *Ibid.*, VIII. xx. 2.   [20] *Ibid.*, VIII. xiii. 5.   [21] *Ibid.*, VIII. xxvii. 2–3.
[22] *Ibid.*, II. xiii. 3–4.   [23] *Epipsychidion*, 379–81.   [24] *Alastor*, 618–19.
[25] *Euganean Hills*, 238.   [26] *Alastor*, 455–56.   [27] *Queen Mab*, v. 22.
[28] *Hellas*, 729–30.   [29] *The Revolt of Islam*, X. xvii. 6–8.

> Before those cruel Twins, whom at one birth
> Incestuous Change bore to her father Time,
> Error and Truth,[30]

Other relations occur; as heirship:

> All that Despair from murdered Hope inherits [31]

Or slavery:

> Eldest of things, divine Equality!
> Wisdom and Love are but the slaves of thee.[32]

> And this was thine, O War! of hate and pain
> Thou loathèd slave [33]

Or partnership:

> Truth with joy enthroned [34]

> Fear is never slow
> To build the thrones of Hate, her mate and foe [35]

Or nutrition:

> Fear,
> The nurse of Vengeance,[36]

Or love:

> But recreant Austria loves thee as the Grave
> Loves Pestilence [37]

Or emanation:

> Justice is the light
> Of love,[38]

Identification is not uncommon. Liberty is identified

---

[30] *The Witch of Atlas*, i. 1–3.
[31] *The Revolt of Islam*, II. vi. 3.
[32] *Ibid.*, V. li. st. 3. ll. 1–2.
[33] *Ibid.*, VI. xvii. 5–6.
[34] *Ibid.*, V. li. st. 6. l. 15.
[35] *Ibid.*, X. xlii. 4–5.
[36] *Ibid.*, IX. xiii. 1–2.
[37] *Hellas*, 312–13.
[38] *The Revolt of Islam*, V. xxxiv. 8–9.

ABSTRACTION

with God's love in the *National Anthem;*[39] in *The Mask of Anarchy,* Freedom is successively identified with Justice, Wisdom, Peace, Love, Spirit, Patience, and Gentleness.[40] To Shelley as to Emerson, all good things were forms of the same good thing.

[39] *A New National Anthem,* iii. 4–7.
[40] Stanzas lvii–lxiv.

Space

AMONG ABSTRACTIONS, Space and Time are remarkable. They have in a high degree what I have noted as the common properties of abstraction, high significance and marked indefiniteness. No ideas are at once more powerful and more indistinct than those of Space and Time. The inference would be that their appeal to Shelley would be extraordinary. Let us see how far this inference is justified.

On at least two distinct occasions Shelley has located the scene of his poem in the pathless supramundane spaces of the Universe. The entire action of the long poem *Queen Mab* takes place in the same region through which Lucifer conducts Cain in Byron's striking drama. The visions of the great *Ode to Liberty* are seen from a point where "the remotest sphere of living flame which paves the void"[1] is flung behind the whirlwind of the ascending spirit. *Prometheus Unbound* includes both Heaven, the abysmal cave of Demogorgon, and places so remote as Caucasus and India among the localities of its action; its fourth act contains a dialogue between the Earth and the Moon.

The Revolt of Islam contains an account in Canto I of a journey from the world of mortals to some not very definitely charted world of redeemed and purified spirits, and in Canto XII a like voyage under other cir-

[1] *Ode to Liberty*, i. 12–13.

cumstances. The space apparently traversed in *Alastor* is remarkable. *The Witch of Atlas* begins in Morocco, includes a highly remote and dimly suggested region called the Austral Lake, and traverses the Nile from Aethiopia to Egypt.² *Hellas,* though observant of the technique of the unities, is throughout European in its scope and embraces America in its concluding outburst. Even *Epipsychidion,* which has no particular occasion for change of place, cannot dispense with "its far Eden of the purple East." There are strong effects of space conveyed in such lyrics as the *Ode to Naples, The Cloud, The Skylark,* the *Ode to the West Wind,* the *Ode to Heaven, The Two Spirits,* and the *Lines written among the Euganean Hills.* Phrases such as "immeasurable sand,"[3] "immeasurable main,"[4] "illimitable plain" (of ocean),[5] "shoreless sea,"[6] "bottomless void,"[7] "hungry space,"[8] "boundless Sea,"[9] "unbounded atmosphere,"[10] "the wide heaven,"[11] "heaven's utmost deep,"[12] "the depth of the unbounded universe,"[13] "unfathomable sky,"[14] "boundless skies,"[15] "wide-wandering stars,"[16] "the stars that wane on the verge of formless space,"[17] "the loftiest star of unascended heaven pinnacled dim in the intense inane,"[18] are both characteristic and decisive.

[2] I. xlvii–xlviii, lvii, etc. See Georg Brandes, *Naturalism in England* (London, 1905), p. 229.
[3] *Queen Mab*, viii. 70. [4] *Alastor*, 279. [5] *Queen Mab*. viii. 89.
[6] *Prometheus Unbound*, III. i. 74. [7] *Ibid.*, III. i. 76. [8] *Ibid.*, IV. 480.
[9] *Epipsychidion*, 420. [10] *Alastor*, 605. [11] *Prometheus Unbound*, II. v. 42.
[12] *Ibid.*, IV. 418. [13] *Queen Mab*, ii. 255.
[14] *Euganean Hills*, 79. [15] *The Revolt of Islam*, V. xv. 7.
[16] *Prometheus Unbound*, II. iv. 88. [17] *The Revolt of Islam*, III. xxvii. 3–4.
[18] *Prometheus Unbound*, III. iv. 203–04.

Shelley can give the effect of prolonged downward movement:

> I sink
> Dizzily down, ever, forever down [19]

Compare also the song of the spirits to the refrain of which Asia and Panthea are conducted to the cave of Demogorgon:

> To the deep, to the deep,
> Down, down! [20]

A mind like this was plainly capable of grasping the thought so exciting to Pascal of the infinity and multitudinousness of the smallest object:

> To whom the fragile blade of grass
> . . . .
> Is an unbounded world.[21]

Or the same idea of the magnitude of the little may be combined, if I have grasped the passage rightly, with the notion of the smallness of the heaven we extol as vast:

> What is heaven? a globe of dew,
> Filling in the morning new
>   Some eyed flower whose young leaves waken
> On an unimagined world;
>   Constellated suns unshaken,
>   Orbits measureless, are furled
>   In that frail and fading sphere,
>   With ten millions gathered there,
>   To tremble, gleam, and disappear.[22]

[19] *Ibid.*, III. i. 80–81.
[20] *Ibid.*, II. iii. 54–55; the whole passage 54–98 is to the point.
[21] *Queen Mab*, ii. 227–30.   [22] *Ode to Heaven*, 46–54.

SPACE

He is capable of strong imaginative effort to grasp the infinity of Space. The subjoined passage illustrates the relative greatness of Adonais and his presumptuous mourners:

> Clasp with thy panting soul the pendulous Earth;
> As from a centre, dart thy spirit's light
> Beyond all worlds, until its spacious might
> Satiate the void circumference; then shrink
> Even to a point within our day and night.[23]

Or again he acknowledges the futility of such efforts:

> This firmament pavilioned upon chaos,
> With all its cressets of immortal fire,
> Whose outwall, bastioned impregnably
> Against the escape of boldest thoughts, repels them.[24]

It should be added that Shelley was very prone to use and very skillful in using those long Latin-sprung adjectives beginning with "in" or "im" or "un," and ending in "able," in which the length of the word and its gradual recession or expiration through a long trail of slowly attenuating syllables are so suggestive of unbounded extension. "Unfathomable," "impenetrable," "illimitable," "immeasurable," "inextricable," are examples.

[23] *Adonais*, xlvii. 3–7.   [24] *Hellas*, 772–75.

Time

SHELLEY's feeling for Space is as vivid as we should expect, but I do not know that it is much stronger than that which is exhibited by equally able and equally sensitive minds of a kindred imaginative bent. His feeling for Time is of a very different intensity. Very few of his imaginative and intellectual equals approach him in the exquisite sensibility, the profound interest, and the full and varied presentation that marked his attitude to this august and mysterious conception. It is easy to trace some, at least, of the grounds of this attraction. Time adds to the impressiveness which, in common with Space, it derives from its infinity, the dramatic interest of movement. Its division into three phases, present, past, and future — of which the first eludes and tantalizes us in the very moment of capture, of which the second is as inaccessible to our regrets as the third is, for the time being, to our longings — endows it with a romantic charm and peculiarity.

As the builder and strengthener of our lives, in the first instance, and later on as their despoiler and underminer, the relation of Time to our own existence possesses a startling contrast and a tragic poignancy distinct from anything to be found among the more neutral and passive attributes of Space; for the consent of humanity has indorsed the fancy of poets in assigning to Time the production of changes which are due in fact to more positive agents. As Shelley's love of classic letters and the life of ancient Greece made him sensitive to the import and glory of the past, so his optimism and his belief in the liberation and purification of humanity made him quick to conceive and vivify the future. These influences aided his keen native sense for what was at the same time momentous and indefinite to generate a sensitiveness to the interest and grandeur of Time almost unequaled in the history of men of letters.

The feeling for Time, however, does not show itself in the temporal extension of his narratives. In this matter, indeed, he is partial to compression. *The Revolt of Islam* includes a blank interval of seven years, but *Alastor* is apparently brief; *The Cenci* can cover, at most, hardly more than a few months, and its effect is even more condensed; the stupendous transactions of *Prometheus Unbound* are completed, as it would seem, in the course of two or three days; and *Hellas* occupies perhaps two hours. On the other hand, *Queen Mab* and the *Ode to Liberty,* the two poems which were cited as examples of Shelley's power of embracing the universe of Space in one perception, must be cited again in illustration of his ability to comprise the whole tract of Time in the compass of a single rapid survey. Both of these poems are, or contain, compendiums of world history.

In discussing Shelley's view of Time, I shall treat chiefly of the general notion (with which that of Eternity may be associated), of its main divisions relative to human experience (present, past, and future), and of the hours and moments. The years, the seasons, the days and nights are of course strictly divisions of Time; but they present themselves to the imagination rather as aspects of nature; the events which mark their rise, fall, and passage are of a nature so concrete and striking that their abstract quality as parcels of duration is lost in this superadded potency. In the Hours and Moments, by an odd paradox, the properties of the great total reappear.

Shelley is prone to speak of Time under physical images, images of stream, flood, storm, and the like:

> the idle foam of Time [1]
>
> the flood of time is rolling on [2]
>
> the flood of ages [3]
>
> the vast stream of ages [4]
>
> Within the surface of Time's fleeting river
> Its wrinkled image lies.[5]
>
> nor the tempest breath of time [6]
>
>   and scorn the storm
> Of time [7]
>
> when the sweeping storm of time
> Has sung its death-dirge o'er the ruined fanes [8]

He compares Time to night:

>   the night of time
> In which suns perished [9]

[1] *Hellas*, 1007.
[2] *The Revolt of Islam*, XII. xxvii. 4.
[3] *Queen Mab*, ii. 254; iii. 142.
[4] *The Revolt of Islam*, II. xii. 5.
[5] *Ode to Liberty*, vi. 1–2.
[6] *Queen Mab*, vi. 227.
[7] *Charles the First*, iv. 52–53.
[8] *Queen Mab*, vi. 220–21.
[9] *Adonais*, v. 4–5.

TIME

Or, with imaginative splendor, to fire:
> And gray walls moulder round, on which dull Time
> Feeds, like slow fire upon a hoary brand [10]

He likens Time to a bird, as
> Both infants weaving wings for time's perpetual way [11]

or with fine suggestiveness,
> Time
> Unfold the brooding pinion of thy gloom [12]

Twice he uses the powerful phrase:
> the heaven of time [13]

The same conception of heaven as the seat of Time is elaborated in the *Ode to Heaven:*
> Of the present and the past
> Of the eternal Where and When,
> Presence-chamber, temple, home,
> Ever-canopying dome
> Of acts and ages yet to come! [14]

Time is personified in various relations. As generator:
> Before those cruel Twins, whom at one birth
> Incestuous Change bore to her father Time,
> Error and Truth,[15]

> My father Time is weak and gray
> With waiting for a better day;
> See how idiot-like he stands,
> Fumbling with his palsied hands! [16]

---

[10] *Ibid.*, l. 1–2. [11] *The Revolt of Islam*, VII. xxi. 9.
[12] *Queen Mab*, viii. 3–4.
[13] *Charles the First*, iv. 56; *A Defence of Poetry*, p. 123.
[14] Lines 5–9. [15] *The Witch of Atlas*, i. 1–3.
[16] *The Mask of Anarchy*, xxiii.

As devourer of his offspring:
>   Time! . . .
> . . . .
>   Render thou up thy half-devoured babes,[17]

As libertine:
>   War with its million horrors, and fierce hell,
>   Shall live but in the memory of time,
>   Who, like a penitent libertine, shall start,
>   Look back, and shudder at his younger years.[18]

Or in the most strangely humanizing and vitalizing appellation that was perhaps ever applied to the vacancy and formlessness of the subject:

> They have been washed in the blood of the mediator and redeemer time [19]

As a scribe or poet:

> They are the episodes of that cyclic poem written by Time upon the memories of men: the past, like an inspired rhapsodist, fills the theatre of everlasting generations with their harmony.[20]

As a corpse:
>   Here, oh, here!
>   We bear the bier
>   Of the Father of many a cancelled year!
>   Spectres we
>   Of the dead Hours be;
>   We bear Time to his tomb in eternity.[21]

As new-born infant:

[17] *Queen Mab*, viii. 3–5. [18] *Ibid.*, v. 256–59.
[19] *A Defence of Poetry*, p. 141. [20] *Ibid.*, p. 121.
[21] *Prometheus Unbound*, IV. 9–14.

TIME

> The thrilling secrets of the birth of time [22]

As pilgrim, with exquisite beauty:

> the faintest sound
> From Time's light footfall [23]

Or in a single brief but profoundly satisfying epithet "restless time." [24] Eternity is also mentioned:

> Adds impotent eternities to pain [25]

He could hardly have missed the Midgard serpent:

> sleep as many-coloured as the snake
> That girds eternity [26]

As with Space, so with Time, he struggles with the impossibility of its realization:

> Yet pause, and plunge
> Into Eternity, where recorded time,
> Even all that we imagine, age on age,
> Seems but a point, and the reluctant mind
> Flags wearily in its unbending flight,
> Till it sink, dizzy, blind, lost, shelterless.[27]

This is followed almost immediately by that noble line in which his spirit transcends the thought that it cannot vanquish:

> Perchance no thought can count them, yet they pass [28]

> Eternity,
> Mother of many acts and hours should free
> The serpent that would clasp her with his length [29]

He has even with unsurpassable audacity ventured in

---

[22] *Alastor*, 128.   [23] *Queen Mab*, iii. 140–41.   [24] *Ibid.*, iii. 20.
[25] *Ibid.*, vii. 250.   [26] *The Revolt of Islam*, iv. 4–5.
[27] *Prometheus Unbound*, I. 416–21.   [28] *Ibid.*, I. 424.   [29] *Ibid.*, IV. 565–67.

effect to introduce Eternity as a character upon his stage:

Jupiter. . . . Awful shape, what art thou? Speak!
Demogorgon. Eternity.[30]

Shelley, like Emerson, was partial to the idea that fullness of experience can impart a virtual infinity to limited portions of Time. It is interesting to find this thought dating back to the composition of *Zastrozzi:*

Days and nights were undistinguished from each other; and the period which he had passed there, though in reality but a few weeks, was lengthened by his perturbed imagination into many years.[31]

Compare the following from *The Revolt of Islam:*

What thoughts had sway o'er Cythna's lonely slumber
That night, I know not; but my own did seem
As if they might ten thousand years outnumber
Of waking life.[32]

The same thought occurs in the same poem (VI. xxxv. 6–9), in a form which would be obscure without an undue lengthening of the citation. It is, once more, nobly phrased in *Epipsychidion,*

make the present last
In thoughts and joys which sleep, but cannot die,
Folded within their own eternity.[33]

Or again in *Queen Mab:*

thoughts that rise
In time-destroying infiniteness, gift

---

[30] *Ibid.,* III. i. 51–52.   [31] *Zastrozzi,* p. 9.
[32] III. i. 1–4.   [33] Lines 522–24.

> With self-enshrined eternity, that mocks
> The unprevailing hoariness of age;[34]

The argument is stated in prose with admirable clearness in an able note on the above passage in *Queen Mab*. The thought is singularly appropriate in the mouth of a poet who made a decade do the work of half a century.

That Shelley should rise to that intellectual metaphysical elevation from which Time and Space are felt to be mere shadows and unrealities is no more than we should have expected from his union of penetration and subtlety.

> The future and the past are idle shadows
> Of thought's eternal flight — they have no being[35]

A poet participates in the eternal, the infinite, and the one; as far as relates to his conceptions, time and place and number are not.[36]

The past and the future are often mentioned by Shelley; the present rarely and chiefly in combination with the others. The three are gracefully associated in the *Epipsychidion,* in a passage of which a part has been already cited:

> I have sent books and music there, and all
> Those instruments with which high spirits call
> The future from its cradle, and the past
> Out of its grave, and make the present last
> In thoughts and joys which sleep, but cannot die,
> Folded within their own eternity.[37]

---

[34] viii. 205–08.
[35] *Hellas,* 783–84.
[36] *A Defence of Poetry,* p. 104.
[37] Lines 519–24.

Similar juxtapositions occur in *Queen Mab*.[38] The same poem speaks of "The secrets of the immeasurable past."[39] The bold figure in which the past is spoken of as an inspired rhapsodist has been already quoted from the *Defence of Poetry*. It is said in *Hellas* to be "like an Incarnation of the To-come," reminding one of Byron's brilliant epigram: "The best of prophets of the future is the past."

The future is characterized in glowing images:

> In the dark Future's ever-flowing urn [40]

Or with picturesque originality:

> the shapes which rove
> Within the homeless Future's wintry grove [41]

Or in a burst of optimism:

> The future, a broad sunrise [42]

Or again in its avenging function:

> the Future, like a snaky scourge,
> Or like some tyrant's eye.[43]

Shelley is perhaps the chief example among recent poets of that prophetic vision which he represents in *A Defence of Poetry* as among the signal endowments and prerogatives of that calling. That *Prometheus Unbound* is formally a recession into the distant and visionary past does not prevent it from being substantially an excursion into the equally distant and perhaps quite as visionary future. Nowhere else has the To-come, as

---

[38] ii. 65–67; viii. 1–3. [39] i. 169. [40] *The Revolt of Islam*, I. xxv. 3.
[41] *Ibid.*, IX. xx. 4–5. [42] *Ibid.*, IX. xxv. 7. [43] *Ibid.*, XI. ix. 6–7.

Shelley calls it, been hymned on so large a scale, with so pure a faith, in a form so poetically exalted. The forward look of his mind is exhibited in *Queen Mab,* also in part prophetic on a cosmic scale; *The Revolt of Islam,* with its projection into the world beyond the grave; *Epipsychidion,* with its closing vision of the still to be attained Ionian Paradise; *Hellas,* with its final canticle to the future splendors of America; and *Adonais,* with the strangely verified forecast of his own doom which brings its inspired strains to their exalted but melancholy conclusion.

Another proof of Shelley's interest in Time is the spell cast upon his fancy by the figure in all romance whose relation to Time is his most conspicuous, most unearthly, and most tragic characteristic. Ahasuerus, the Wandering Jew, is called up to assail Christianity in the earliest of Shelley's long works, *Queen Mab,* and reappears to conjure up the ghost of Mahomet before the eyes of the discomfited and despairing Mahmud in *Hellas,* the last long work which he completed.

I proceed to the discussion of Shelley's handling of Hours and Moments. Hours, as is well known, are much more than the subjects of casual allusion and personification in Shelley, important as their place is even in this secondary function. They are brought upon the stage as singing, speaking, acting characters. In the fourth act of *Prometheus Unbound* there is a chorus of "past hours weak and grey," who sing an antiphony with a chorus of spirits, and whose sections answer each other in responsive strophes. In the second act the hour of Jupiter's downfall is embodied in a shape of terror and utters a baleful prophecy. The spirit of the hour of deliverance, in an "ivory shell inlaid with crimson fire," with its "dove-like eyes of hope," plays a part of some importance, including one speech of one hundred and six lines, in the second and third acts. I know of no other poet who has duplicated or even approached a performance of this kind. When Milton has said "The Graces, and the rosy-bosom'd Hours, thither all their bounties bring," when Collins has said "The fragrant Hours and Elves who slept in buds the day," both are satisfied that mere Hours have been adequately, even generously, dealt with. To Shelley an Hour was as distinct and vivific as a day or a night to other poets.

The following passage is of interest in this place:

> The rocks are cloven, and through the purple night
> I see cars drawn by rainbow-wingèd steeds
> Which trample the dim winds; in each there stands
> A wild-eyed charioteer urging their flight.
> Some look behind, as fiends pursued them there,
> And yet I see no shapes but the keen stars;
> Others, with burning eyes, lean forth, and drink
> With eager lips the wind of their own speed,
> As if the thing they loved fled on before,
> And now, even now, they clasped it. Their bright locks
> Stream like a comet's flashing hair; they all
> Sweep onward.[44]

Reading this glowing and palpitant passage, in the absence of its context, which is sometimes cited as an ex-

[44] *Prometheus Unbound*, II. iv. 129–40.

TIME 27

ample of Shelley's descriptive power, who could imagine that the actors in this fiery carnival were those petty and commonplace divisions of Time which most of us associate with nothing more exciting than the leisurely progress of a small steel bar around a disk of graduated paper?

There are other images. The Hours are tenderly conceived, as in this from *The Sensitive Plant:*

> While the lagging hours of the day went by
> Like windless clouds o'er a tender sky.[45]

Or once more, with animation and passion:

> The eager hours and unreluctant years
> As on a dawn-illumined mountain stood,
> Trampling to silence their loud hopes and fears,
> Darkening each other with their multitude,[46]

Or as ghosts:

> Spectres we
> Of the dead Hours be;
> We bear Time to his tomb in eternity.[47]

> I call the phantoms of a thousand hours,
> Each from his voiceless grave [48]

Sometimes to ghostliness terror and sublimity are annexed:

> those dead but unforgotten hours,
> Where ghosts scare victor kings in their ancestral towers.[49]

It is worth noting, parenthetically, that the Day is also figured as a ghost; with power in *Adonais:*

[45] i. 96–97. [46] *Ode to Liberty*, xi. 1–4. [47] *Prometheus Unbound*, IV. 12–14.
[48] *Hymn to Intellectual Beauty*, vi. 4–5. [49] *Ode to Liberty*, xii. 14–15.

> The golden Day, which, on eternal wings,
> Even as a ghost abandoning a bier,
> Had left the Earth a corpse;[50]

The Hour is somberly or sadly depicted:

> And thou, sad Hour, selected from all years
> To mourn our loss, rouse thy obscure compeers,
> And teach them thine own sorrow![51]

> Ask the cold, pale Hour,
> Rich in reversion of impending death,[52]

Or with mystery combined with sadness:

> but the unborn hour,
> Cradled in fear and hope, conflicting storms,
> Who shall unveil?[53]

Or with gloomy and daring imagery:

> to whom once this present hour,
> This gloomy crag of time to which I cling,
> Seemed an Elysian isle of peace and joy
> Never to be attained.[54]

Or with the note of weariness:

> a heavy weight of hours[55]

> Day after day, a weary waste of hours[56]

Or in the act of inducing oblivion:

> and when years heap
> Their withered hours, like leaves, on our decay[57]

The intensity of his personification, or rather vitalization, takes a further step; the Hours become fierce:

[50] *Adonais,* xxiii. 3–5. [51] *Ibid.,* i. 4–6. [52] *Hellas,* 902–03.
[53] *Ibid.,* 752–54. [54] *Ibid.,* 925–28. [55] *Ode to the West Wind,* iv. 13.
[56] *Alastor,* 245. [57] *Epipsychidion,* 536–37.

TIME

> Once the hungry Hours were hounds
> Which chased the day like a bleeding deer [58]

> Oh, that the hour when present had cast off
> The mantle of its mystery, and shown
> The ghastly form with which it now returns
> When its scared game is roused, cheering the hounds
> Of conscience to their prey! [59]

In one remarkable passage the Hour becomes clothed in the most solemn and terrible attributes of humanity, and is vivified to an all but incredible intensity:

> for then they lead
> The wingless, crawling hours, one among whom —
> As some dark Priest hales the reluctant victim —
> Shall drag thee, cruel King, to kiss the blood
> From these pale feet,[60]

This sums up the significant evidence as to Hours; it is just worth mentioning that flowers are twice designated by the graceful title of "children of the hours." [61] In the last quotation from *Prometheus Unbound* the Hours are spoken of as wingless and crawling. The same words are applied to moments in another passage of the poem: "How like death-worms the wingless moments crawl!" [62] By a daring hyperbole he extends the notion of infinity to moments:

> making moments be
> As mine seem, — each an immortality! [63]

---

[58] *Prometheus Unbound*, IV. 73–74.
[59] *The Cenci*, V. i. 5–9.
[60] *Prometheus Unbound*, I. 47–51.
[61] *Song of Proserpine*, ii. 4; *The Question*, v. 5.
[62] II. i. 16.
[63] *Julian and Maddalo*, 418–19.

The Mind : The Passions

AMONG FACTS of profound import and indefinite or impalpable substance none are more conspicuous than mind and its contents. Nothing combines potency and elusiveness more signally than thought. If feeling is slightly less elusive, it is even more potent. Shelley could hardly fail to be deeply sensitive to both of these mysterious and mighty phenomena. To him thought as thought, feeling as feeling, apart from their subject or content, apart from their relation to his own happiness or the movement of events in the outside world, were perennially and intensely interesting. Of the passions I say little, because the topic is in part identical with the abstractions already handled, and the reader who wishes copious illustration is referred to the discussion of that subject. A few points may be made, and briefly exemplified.

Phrases like "pain and fear and hate,"[1] "hate and pride and fear,"[2] "a winged sound of joy and love and wonder,"[3] "wisdom, courage, and long-suffering love,"[4] "ministers of pain, and fear, and disappointment, and mistrust, and hate, and clinging crime,"[5] "mutinous passions and conflicting fears, and hopes that sate themselves on dust and die"[6] illustrate both the liveliness of

[1] *The Revolt of Islam*, XII. xi. 2.
[2] *To a Skylark*, 92.
[3] *Ode to Liberty*, vi. 9.
[4] *Prometheus Unbound*, III. iii. 2.
[5] *Ibid.*, I. 452–54.
[6] *Hellas*, 884–85.

THE MIND: THE PASSIONS

Shelley's interest in the passions and his propensity, previously noted or implied, for listing them in files or bunching them in clusters. He felt an eloquence in their very names. I am not sure that in Shelley's mind the ordinary process of conduction or vivification was not reversed, that the passion did not do more to vitalize the individual than the individual to substantiate the passion. I have already spoken of his habit of relating abstractions to one another by parental, fraternal, or social bonds, and the passions play so large a part in the illustrations previously offered that repetition at this point would be futile and tedious.

Presentation of Mind in Terms of Matter

THE ILLUSTRATION of mental facts by physical images is a phenomenon that reaches back into the origins of language. When a name for the mental fact is wanted, it is found in the appropriation to the new purpose of the name of a physical fact. Carlyle pointed out the imaginative moment in the early history of the race in which the idea of stretching out was first applied, in the glow of metaphor, to the mental habit of attention. Words like "spirit," "right," and "wrong" are hackneyed instances of this familiar transference. When we wish to think vividly of mind, we are obliged to ask matter to help us.

It would be a mistake, however, to suppose that because illustrations of this kind are deeply inwoven in the texture of our language they are involved to any like extent in the tissues of our thinking. The power to originate illustrations of mind through matter is by no means a universal or even a common one: the very words of which I have been speaking, in spite of their apparent witness to its generality, were the inspirations of rare minds in creative moments; and their propagation was only the sign of the inability of the masses to originate the felicities they pilfered. In early and even in fairly mature periods there is no occasion to think of mind in terms of matter for the simple reason that there is no wish to think of mind at all. Men are like children before a looking glass; it is a long time before their thoughts turn from the *image* to the *mirror*. Even the great minds of primitive epochs share the incapacity.

It is, of course, not the degree of imagination or genius but the degree of introspection or self-scrutiny that measures the exercise of this power. As nations come to refine and to analyze the usage broadens. Certain obvious analogies, the likening of purity to whiteness, of evil to stain, of lust or wrath to fire, of wrath again to flood, of pitilessness to iron or marble, of pliability to wax, become universal, semi-proverbial; and there are functions of growth and decay, of digestion and assimilation, of forward and backward vision, of exaltation and depression, of wandering, of paralysis, in which body and mind are so much alike that the likeness insists on being recognized in speech and writing. Even today, however, the origination of this kind of figure would mark a mind as somewhat above the common; and even among men of the first rank, any unusual fertility or energy in this respect confers a species of distinction, though the passage of each new decade in a self-probing and self-sophisticating age deprives the distinction of a part of its rarity. I do not affirm that Shelley surpassed Coleridge, or Emerson, or Hawthorne, or George Eliot in this respect, but the tendency and the faculty were developed in his intelligence to a remarkable degree — a degree which, striking in itself, is doubly striking when viewed in connection with the fact that his poetry has rarely been credited with psychological or intellectual mastery. That he should altogether excel Scott, the poet of externals, is nothing; that he should excel Byron greatly is little; but that he should at least equal Wordsworth, a poet of admittedly introspective and meditative tendency is a fact of distinguished interest. That this equality is real, I believe the following illustrations will make clear.

The images under which the mind or heart or soul is presented as a unit are of singular power and variety:

> that black and dreary bell, the soul,
> Hung in a heaven-illumined tower, must toll [1]

The soul is likened to a judgment-seat:

> the judgment-throne
> Of its own aweless soul [2]

The mind, more conventionally, is compared to a temple:

> Hypocrisy and custom make their minds
> The fanes of many a worship now outworn.[3]

The same figure is coupled with powerful personification of the will:

> And like a suppliant in some gorgeous fane,
> Let the will kneel within thy haughty breast [4]

Or with striking originality, the soul is likened to a standard:

> Tomb of Arminius! render up thy dead

---

[1] *Julian and Maddalo*, 123–24. [2] *Ode to Liberty*, xvi. 7–8.
[3] *Prometheus Unbound*, I. 621–22. [4] *Ibid.*, I. 377–78.

MIND IN TERMS OF MATTER

>   Till, like a standard from a watch-tower's staff,
>   His soul may stream over the tyrant's head; [5]

The above images are derived from artificial objects; those taken from nature are quite as remarkable. The heart becomes a vine:

>   and Love he sent to bind
>   The disunited tendrils of that vine
>   Which bears the wine of life, the human heart [6]

The mind becomes a sun:

>   within whose mind sits peace serene
>   As light in the sun, throned [7]

The figures often convey the idea of bulk or extent to a degree not usual in imagery applied to the mind. "Thought's wildernesses" are spoken of in *Prometheus Unbound*.[8] The mind is likened to an ocean, a heaven:

>   We come from the mind
>   Of humankind,
>   Which was late so dusk, and obscene, and blind;
>   Now 'tis an ocean
>   Of clear emotion,
>   A heaven of serene and mighty motion.[9]

>   Hark, sister! what a low yet dreadful groan
>   Quite unsuppressed is tearing up the heart
>   Of the good Titan, as storms tear the deep,
>   And beasts hear the sea moan in inland caves.[10]

Compare, though here the thought is treated in a somewhat different way:

[5] *Ode to Liberty*, xiv. 1–3.
[7] *Ibid.*, I. 430–31.
[9] *Ibid.*, IV. 93–98.
[6] *Prometheus Unbound*, II. iv. 63–65.
[8] *Ibid.*, I. 742.
[10] *Ibid.*, I. 578–81.

> But Greece and her foundations are
> Built below the tide of war,
> Based on the crystalline sea
> Of thought and its eternity;[11]

Shelley is prone to represent the human mind as the sea-beach imprinted by the passing waves of consciousness. So with much beauty in *The Sensitive Plant:*

> And the beasts, and the birds, and the insects were drowned
> In an ocean of dreams without a sound,
> Whose waves never mark, though they ever impress
> The light sand which paves it, consciousness;[12]

> my brain became as sand
> Where the first wave had more than half erased
> The track of deer on desert Labrador,[13]

> Not until my dream became
> Like a child's legend on the tideless sand,
> Which the first foam erases half, and half
> Leaves legible.[14]

Thought's "world-surrounding aether" is spoken of in *Prometheus Unbound.*[15] A little later the idea is strikingly elaborated with imagery unexcelled for melancholy picturesqueness:

> And we breathe, and sicken not,
> The atmosphere of human thought:
> Be it dim, and dank, and gray,
> Like a storm-extinguished day,
> Travelled o'er by dying gleams;
> Be it bright as all between
> Cloudless skies and windless streams,

[11] *Hellas,* 696–99. [12] i. 102–05. [13] *The Triumph of Life,* 405–07.
[14] *Fragments of an Unfinished Drama,* 151–54. [15] I. 661.

MIND IN TERMS OF MATTER

    Silent, liquid, and serene;
As the birds within the wind,
  As the fish within the wave,
As the thoughts of man's own mind
    Float through all above the grave;
We make there our liquid lair,
Voyaging cloudlike and unpent
Through the boundless element: [16]

The curious intimacy of association between matter and spirit in Shelley's mind is notably evinced in lines 683–86, where material and spiritual objects (birds, fish, thoughts) are not only felt to be susceptible of comparison with each other but are bunched or bracketed together as kindred materials from which comparisons may be applied in groups to other things. But more on this topic below.

Of all figures from nature the most frequent, and the most remarkable in their frequency, are those drawn from caverns or caves. Shelley's keen sense of the secrecy, the dimness, and the intricacy of the human mind appears to have satisfied itself in a persistent reversion to this image.

                  those subtle and fair spirits,
Whose homes are the dim caves of human thoughts [17]

Which thro' the deep and labyrinthine soul,
Like echoes, thro' long caverns, wind and roll [18]

           a friend's bosom
Is as the inmost cave of our own mind [19]

[16] *Prometheus Unbound*, I. 675–89.   [17] *Ibid.*, I. 658–59.
[18] *Ibid.*, I. 805–06.   [19] *The Cenci*, II. ii. 88–89.

> the inmost cave
> Of man's deep spirit [20]
>
> Within a cavern of man's trackless spirit [21]
>
> the caverns dreary and forlorn
> Of the riven soul [22]
>
> "My mind became the book through which I grew
> Wise in all human wisdom, and its cave,
> Which like a mine I rifled through and through,
> To me the keeping of its secrets gave — " [23]
>
> the caverns of the spirit [24]

In two places ideas of richness and magnificence are associated with those of mystery and intricacy:

> Each pursues what seems most fair,
> Mining, like moles, through mind, and there
> Scoop palace-caverns vast, where Care
> In thronèd state is ever dwelling.[25]
>
> From that deep abyss
> Of wonder and bliss
> Whose caverns are crystal palaces;
> From those skyey towers
> Where Thought's crowned powers
> Sit watching your dance, ye happy Hours! [26]

In *The Triumph of Life* the mind is likened, eccentrically, to embers:

> all the gazer's mind was strewn beneath
> Her feet like embers [27]

[20] *Ode to Liberty*, xviii. 1–2.
[22] *The Revolt of Islam*, III. xxii. 3–4.
[24] *A Defence of Poetry*, p. 139.
[26] *Prometheus Unbound*, IV. 99–104.
[21] *Ibid.*, canceled passage, 1.
[23] *Ibid.*, VII. xxxi. 1–4.
[25] *Peter Bell the Third*, III. xxiii.
[27] Lines 386–87.

MIND IN TERMS OF MATTER

The soul is compared to a fawn, with recurrence of the cave-metaphor,

> And so his soul would not be gay,
> But moaned within him; like a fawn
> Moaning within a cave, it lay [28]

In the oceanic and atmospheric imagery we saw Shelley picturing mind under images uniting vastness with simplicity. Sometimes extent is joined with complication:

> Which hid in one dim gulf the troubled stream
> Of mind, a boundless chaos wild and vast [29]

The cosmic aspect of the human mind was certain not to escape an intuition so exquisite. In *Epipsychidion* the term "frail Universe" is applied to his own heart.[30] To compare the mind to a world is common enough, but the specifications in this passage are not ordinary:

> Twin Spheres of light who rule this passive Earth,
> This world of love, this *me;* and into birth
> Awaken all its fruits and flowers, and dart
> Magnetic might into its central heart;
> And lift its billows and its mists, and guide
> By everlasting laws each wind and tide
> To its fit cloud, and its appointed cave;
> And lull its storms, each in the craggy grave
> Which was its cradle, luring to faint bowers
> The armies of the rainbow-wingèd showers; [31]

Even here it will be observed that the cave is specified. In a similar passage the term Paradise is employed:

[28] *Peter Bell the Third,* VI. xxx. 1–3.
[20] Line 369.
[29] *The Revolt of Islam,* III. i. 5–6.
[31] *Epipsychidion,* 345–54.

> thine own heart — it is a Paradise
> Which everlasting spring has made its own,
> And while drear winter fills the naked skies,
> Sweet streams of sunny thought, and flowers fresh blown,
> Are there, and weave their sounds and odours into one.[32]

The above illustrations regard the mind as a unit; in those which follow its parts are presented as aggregates or multitudes, a conception in which Shelley's love of magnitude is almost as plain as in the foregoing figures.

> To feed my many thoughts: a tameless multitude [33]

> had my song
> Peopled with thoughts the boundless universe,
> A mighty congregation.[34]

> this undistinguishable mist
> Of thoughts, which rise, like shadow after shadow,
> Darkening each other? [35]

> and make his youth
> The sepulchre of hope, where evil thoughts
> Shall grow like weeds on a neglected tomb.[36]

> a throng
> Of thoughts and forms [37]

Sometimes, by a noteworthy modification, the figures are military:

> Prometheus saw, and waked the legioned hopes
> Which sleep within folded Elysian flowers [38]

[32] *The Revolt of Islam*, IX. xxvi. 5–9.   [33] *Ibid.*, II. ix. 9.
[34] *Ibid.*, II. xxx. 1–3.   [35] *The Cenci*, III. i. 170–72.   [36] *Ibid.*, IV. i. 52–54.
[37] *Prometheus Unbound*, IV. 416–17.   [38] *Ibid.*, II. iv. 59–60.

MIND IN TERMS OF MATTER 41

became as generals to the bewildered armies of their thoughts [39]

> One legion of wild thoughts [40]

The power to convey multitude and to personify with vigor the constitutents of the multitude is manifest in the following:

> The world I say of thoughts that worshipped her.[41]

The treatment of separate passions or ideas remains to be considered. In the Furies and the so-called Spirits of the first act of the *Prometheus* Shelley employs an extraordinary, perhaps an unparalleled, mode of personification. The beings thus introduced are apparently not embodiments of passions, such as the Hate, Wrath, Pride, and Jealousy with which literature has, somewhat to our cost, familiarized us, but the incarnations of experiences, of particular moments or sensations in the growth or activity of passion. This accounts for their number and their marked individuality. The Furies compare themselves to a "vain loud multitude" and threaten to

> be dread thought, beneath thy brain,
> And foul desire round thine astonished heart.[42]

The gracious spirits breathe "the atmosphere of human thought," are likewise a thronging troop, and represent, as it would seem, isolated and specialized experiences. Impalpable as the conception may appear, and unusual as it certainly is, the chants of these latter not

---
[39] *A Defence of Poetry*, p. 122.   [40] *Mont Blanc*, 41.
[41] *Epipsychidion*, 245.   [42] *Prometheus Unbound*, I. 488–89.

42 POWER AND ELUSIVENESS IN SHELLEY

only include some of the proudest claims which English lyric can put forth to an immortality of glory, but exhibit Shelley's lyrical gift in its most concrete and definite, and therefore in its sanest and soundest, manifestation. The passage is too long to quote, and too beautiful not to be familiar.

The curious faculty of giving life and personality to individual thoughts is shown in the following passages:

> must toll
> Our thoughts and our desires to meet below
> Round the rent heart and pray — as mad-men do
> For what? they know not [43]
>
> Till human thoughts might kneel alone
> Each before the judgment throne [44]

The canceled passage in the *Ode to Liberty* also mentions "thoughts that kneel and tremble." The following passages are similar, with a difference:

> there is a secret known
> To thee, and to none else of living things,
> Which may transfer the sceptre of wide Heaven,
> The fear of which perplexes the Supreme.
> Clothe it in words, and bid it clasp his throne
> In intercession; bend thy soul in prayer,
> And like a suppliant in some gorgeous fane,
> Let the will kneel within thy haughty heart,[45]
>
> Because I am a priest do you believe
> Your image, as the hunter some struck deer,
> Follows me not whether I wake or sleep? [46]

[43] *Julian and Maddalo*, 124–27.
[45] *Prometheus Unbound*, I. 371–78.
[44] *Ode to Liberty*, xvi. 6–7.
[46] *The Cenci*, I. ii. 11–13.

And his own thoughts, along that rigged way,
Pursued, like raging hounds, their father and their prey.[47]

The longer passage in *Adonais* (Cantos IX–XIII) is really amazing. The subjects of personification in this case are poetical fancies, motives, or conceptions, which Shelley idealizes under such names as Dreams, Ministers of thought:

> Desires and Adorations,
> Wingèd Persuasions and veiled Destinies,
> Splendours, and Glooms, and glimmering Incarnations
> Of hopes and fears, and twilight Phantasies;
> And Sorrow, with her family of Sighs,
> And Pleasure,[48]

These ideas speak, weep, clasp the poet's head, throw wreaths, clip their own locks, break bows and arrows, wash his limbs.

> And one with trembling hand clasps his cold head,
> And fans him with her moonlight wings, and cries,
> "Our love, our hope, our sorrow, is not dead;
> See, on the silken fringe of his faint eyes,
> Like dew upon a sleeping flower, there lies
> A tear some Dream has loosened from his brain."
> Lost Angel of a ruined Paradise!
> She knew not 'twas her own; as with no stain
> She faded, like a cloud which had outwept its rain.

> One from a lucid urn of starry dew
> Washed his light limbs, as if enbalming them;
> Another clipped her profuse locks, and threw
> The wreath upon him, like an anadem,
> Which frozen tears instead of pearls begem;

[47] *Adonais*, xxxi. 8–9.   [48] *Ibid.*, xiii. 1–6.

Another in her wilful grief would break
Her bow and wingèd reeds, as if to stem
A greater loss with one which was more weak;
And dull the barbèd fire against his frozen cheek.[49]

As a parallel passage to parts of the five stanzas Mr. Forman cites *Rosalind and Helen,*

a winged band
Of bright Persuasions, which had fed
On his sweet lips and liquid eyes,[50]

There are other cases in which the imagery, usually dealing with specific passions or sentiments, falls short of personification. Joy and peace are figured as light,

within whose mind sits peace serene
As light in the sun, throned [51]

Thou art folded, thou art lying
In the light which is undying
Of thine own joy,[52]

Ha! ha! the animation of delight
Which wraps me, like an atmosphere of light,
And bears me as a cloud is borne by its own wind.[53]

veiled in the light
Of the desire that makes thee one with me [54]

Here is a conceit of an extravagance quite Elizabethan. The subject is "two runnels":

like sisters
Who part with sighs that they may meet in smiles,
Turning their dear disunion to an isle
Of lovely grief, a wood of sweet sad thoughts;[55]

---

[49] *Adonais,* x–xi.   [50] Lines 746–48.   [51] *Prometheus Unbound,* I. 430–31.
[52] *Ibid.,* IV. 437–39.   [53] *Ibid.,* IV. 322–24.   [54] *Ibid.,* III. i. 34–35.
[55] *Ibid.,* IV. 198–201.

MIND IN TERMS OF MATTER

Compare the above puerility with the splendid and terrific vigor of the following:

> The hope of torturing him smells like a heap
> Of corpses, to a death-bird after battle [56]

The Earth, in characterizing her own pride, does not balk at the stupendous hyperbole, "my pride's deep universe." [57] The mightiest and most intangible qualities are figured under the most concrete and poignant usages:

> I curse thee! let a sufferer's curse
> Clasp thee, his torturer, like remorse;
> Till thine Infinity shall be
> A robe of envenomed agony;
> And thine Omnipotence a crown of pain,
> To cling like burning gold round thy dissolving brain! [58]

The comparisons of words to "a cloud of winged snakes" [59] and of lies pursuing their victim "as hooded ounces cling to the driven hind" [60] are interesting, but do not fall strictly, or at least not entirely, within the scope of our present purpose.

We have observed, then, Shelley's power of conceiving the whole mind, the mind as a unit, in vivid material images, sometimes drawn from art, more often from nature, often vast in extent, sometimes cosmic in their complexity and abundance; his power of imaging the multitude of individual thoughts or sensations; the energy and originality of personification which extends even to objects so small and so featureless, according to

[56] *Ibid.*, I. 339–40. [57] *Ibid.*, IV. 500. [58] *Ibid.*, I. 286–91.
[59] *Ibid.*, I. 632. [60] *Ibid.*, I. 609.

everyday notions, as particular thoughts; and lastly the vivid images under which specific passions or properties are materialized. We have seen that he was deeply sensitive to the infinity of mind, to its complication, to its mystery, to the manifoldness of the objects that people it. I conclude with a passage from one of Shelley's manuscripts preserved for us in Mrs. Shelley's "Note on *Prometheus Unbound*."

In the Greek Shakespeare, Sophocles, we find the image,
Πολλὰς δ' ὁδοὺς ἐλθόντα φροντίδος πλάνοις :
a line of almost unfathomable depth of poetry; yet how simple are the images in which it is arrayed!

"Coming to many ways in the wanderings of careful thought." If the words ὁδοὺς and πλάνοις had not been used, the line might have been explained in a metaphorical instead of an absolute sense, as we say "*ways* and means," and "wanderings" for error and confusion. But they meant literally paths or roads, such as we tread with our feet; and wanderings, such as a man makes when he loses himself in a desert, or roams from city to city — as Œdipus, the speaker of this verse, was destined to wander, blind and asking charity. What a picture does this line suggest of the mind as a wilderness of intricate paths, wide as the universe, which is here made its symbol; a world within a world which he who seeks some knowledge with respect to what he ought to do searches throughout, as he would search the external universe for some valued thing which was hidden from him upon its surface.

Presentation of Matter in Terms of Mind

IN THE PREFACE to *Prometheus Unbound* Shelley says:

> The imagery which I have employed will be found, in many instances, to have been drawn from the operations of the human mind, or from those external actions by which they are expressed. This is unusual in modern poetry, although Dante and Shakespeare are full of instances of the same kind; Dante indeed more than any other poet, and with greater success. But the Greek poets, as writers to whom no resource of awakening the sympathy of their contemporaries was unknown, were in the habitual use of this power; and it is the study of their works (since a higher merit would probably be denied me) to which I am willing that my readers should impute this singularity.

Shelley was quite right in calling the practice on which he touches in the above paragraph unusual. To illustrate mental facts by material imagery is perfectly natural to anyone who has attained that level of self-consciousness in which the study of mental facts for their own sake is a means of pleasure: it is the outgrowth of that common and rational instinct which impels us to relate the dark to the clear, the indefinite to the precise, the less known to the better known. Every one of these motives is opposed to the reverse process of the illustration of matter from intellectual or moral data. Knowledge gains much in clearness and vividness by its association with the idea of light, but light gains nothing, or at least nothing of comparable worth, by association with the idea of knowledge. Few people have found the twilight of mind a source of useful illustrations for the noonday of matter; and perhaps the greatest proof that a man can offer of reality, distinctness, and intensity in the view he takes of mind is his application of images derived from that source to the elucidation of material phenomena. The habitual practice of this art is a point in which it seems to me that Shelley is more than remarkable, that he is very nearly, if not quite, unique among the better and better-known representatives of letters.

The images are often drawn from thoughts:

From all the blasts of heaven thou hast descended;
Yes, like a spirit, like a thought,[1]

Sculptures, like life and thought, immovable, deep-eyed [2]

Couched on the fountain like a panther tame,
. . . .
Or on blind Homer's heart a wingèd thought, —
In joyous expectation lay the boat.[3]

Morn, noon and even, that boat of pearl outran
    The streams which bore it, like the arrowy cloud
Of tempest, or the speedier thought of man,[4]

Observe in the last two examples the association, not rare in Shelley, of a sensuous and a supersensuous

[1] *Prometheus Unbound*, II. i. 1–2. [2] *The Revolt of Islam*, I. li. 9.
[3] *The Witch of Atlas*, xxxiv. 4–8. [4] *The Revolt of Islam*, XII. xxxv. 1–3.

MATTER IN TERMS OF MIND

image, the former ushering the latter. This apposition of mind and matter is almost as significant as their express conjunction. The habit is beautifully illustrated in the following, in which the idea of the man's thought in the infant's brain is one of those elusively delicate conceptions which the Shelleys of the world alone can trace to their mysterious lurking-places:

> And, like unfolded flowers beneath the sea,
>   Like the man's thought dark in the infant's brain,
> Like aught that is which wraps what is to be,
>   Art's deathless dreams lay veiled by many a vein
> Of Parian stone;[5]

> The Champak odours fail
> Like sweet thoughts in a dream [6]

> swifter than thought [7]

> And your wings are soft and swift as thought
> And your eyes are as love which is veilèd not [8]

Here is a case in which a natural phenomenon peculiarly associated with those ideas of mass and momentum which seem least harmonious with mind is reinforced by immaterial images:

>   Hark! the rushing snow!
> The sun-awakened avalanche! whose mass,
> Thrice sifted by the storm, had gathered there
> Flake after flake, in heaven-defying minds
> As thought by thought is piled, till some great truth
> Is loosened, and the nations echo round,[9]

[5] *Ode to Liberty*, IV. 9–13.   [6] *An Indian Serenade*, ii. 3–4.
[7] *Prometheus Unbound*, IV. 275.   [8] *Ibid.*, IV. 91–92.
[9] *Ibid.*, II. iii. 36–41.

Dreams, referred to in two of the quotations above, supply additional illustrations:

> thou dost wake, O Spring!
> O child of many winds! As suddenly
> Thou comest as the memory of a dream,
> Which now is sad because it hath been sweet;
> Like genius, or like joy [10]

Observe the tendency to mass images of this sort, as in the memory of a dream, the genius and the joy of the above passage.

> tyrants would flee
> Like a dream's dim imagery [11]

> shades beautiful and white,
> Amid sweet sounds across our path would sweep,
> Like swift and lovely dreams that walk the waves of sleep.[12]

The heart and soul become the subjects of imagery, as in these lines from *Alastor:*

> Hither the Poet came. His eyes beheld
> Their own wan light through the reflected lines
> Of his thin hair, distinct in the dark depth
> Of that still fountain; as the human heart,
> Gazing in dreams over the gloomy grave,
> Sees its own treacherous likeness there.[13]

The following is an example of Shelley's occasional willingness to pursue a conceit until it sinks down exhausted and of the curious device of illustrating by a metaphysical image a physical fact which is no fact but only an extravagance of fancy. The Lady speaks of a

[10] *Ibid.*, II. i. 6–10.
[11] *The Mask of Anarchy*, lii. 3–4.
[12] *The Revolt of Islam*, XII. xxxvi. 7–9.
[13] Lines 469–74.

mysterious plant raised from something that looked like melon seeds:

> Its leaves were delicate, you almost saw
> The pulses
> With which the purple velvet flower was fed
> To overflow, and, like a poet's heart
> Changing bright fancy to sweet sentiment,
> Changed half the light to fragrance.[14]

In *The Cenci* we have a famous passage in which the temptation to draw upon the supersensuous world for a powerful image overcomes the weight not only of the dramatic proprieties of the occasion but of Shelley's own avowed practice and purpose throughout the remainder of that un-Shelleyan drama. How great the power of the passage must be is evinced in the forgiveness which it wins for its signal departure from dramatic fitness.

> And in its depth there is a mighty rock,
> Which has, from unimaginable years,
> Sustained itself with terror and with toil
> Over a gulf, and with the agony
> With which it clings seems slowly coming down;
> Even as a wretched soul hour after hour
> Clings to the mass of life; yet clinging, leans;
> And, leaning, makes more dark the dread abyss
> In which it fears to fall; beneath this crag
> Huge as despair, as if in weariness,
> The melancholy mountain yawns;[15]

Observe that the main simile, the likeness of the rock to the despairing soul, is supplemented by another, the

[14] *Fragments of an Unfinished Drama*, 172–77.   [15] III. i. 247–57.

likeness of the cleft in the mountain to the yawn of weariness, a fancy which might perhaps strike us as a descent but for the all-atoning resonance and expressiveness of the sounds in which the idea is conveyed.

Another passage in *The Cenci,* in which the greatest vigor of phrase is combined with the strictest dramatic suitability, lies on the border, as it were, of the present topic. When the guards separate Bernardo from Beatrice, he exclaims:

> Oh! would ye divide
> Body from soul? [16]

The passions also are invoked:

> The heaped waves behold
> The deep calm of blue heaven dilating above,
> And, like passions made still by the presence of Love,
> Beneath the clear surface reflecting it slide
> Tremulous with soft influence; [17]

music sweet as love [18]

So that her way was paved, and roofed above
With flowers as soft as thoughts of budding love [19]

And when evening descended from heaven above,
And the Earth was all rest, and the air was all love [20]

> Away, unlovely dreams!
> Away, false shapes of sleep!
> Be his, as Heaven seems,
> Clear, and bright, and deep!
> Soft as love, and calm as death,[21]

---

[16] V. iii. 94–95.
[17] *A Vision of the Sea,* 128–32.
[18] *To a Skylark,* 45.
[19] *Epipsychidion,* 327–28.
[20] *The Sensitive Plant,* i. 98–99.
[21] *Hellas,* 8–12.

MATTER IN TERMS OF MIND

With his characteristic fashion of coupling the material with the non-material Shelley goes on in the next line of the foregoing passage to wish the desired sleep to be "Sweet as a summer night without a breath."

Compare with this delicate if airy effect the infelicitous accumulation and diversification of images in the following passage, in which the spirits exhaust themselves in the effort to find similes for the downward movement of Asia and Panthea into the cave of Demogorgon:

> As the fawn draws the hound,
> As the lightning the vapor,
> As a weak moth the taper;
> Death, despair; love, sorrow;
> Time, both; to-day, to-morrow;
> As steel obeys the spirit of the stone.[22]

Joy, used above to express the descent of Spring, is found again in one of the incomparable lines of the *Skylark:*

> In the golden lightning
> Of the sunken sun,
> O'er which clouds are bright'ning,
> Thou dost float and run;
> Like an unbodied joy whose race is just begun.[23]

The "isle of lovely grief," the "wood of sweet sad thoughts,"[24] cited above must not be overlooked in this context.

> Our feet now, every palm
> Are sandalled with calm [25]

---
[22] *Prometheus Unbound,* II. iii. 65-70.
[24] *Prometheus Unbound,* IV. 200-01. See page 44 above.
[23] Lines 11-15.
[25] *Ibid.,* IV. 123-24.

they come —
Blackening the birth of day with countless wings,
And hollow underneath, like death.[26]

This terminates my citations. It will be observed that only a few of the figures quoted in this section (the extracts from *The Cenci* more particularly) are distinctively powerful, that many are merely acceptable, and that several are unmistakably weak. The inference as to the value of such figures in hands less accomplished than Shelley's seems tolerably clear. The very incompleteness of his success, however, is another proof of the extraordinary nature of that fascination which led him to draw so many images from a source which scarcely repaid his diligence. He loved mind, soul, thoughts, dreams, passions, and made excuses, where he could not find justifications, for recurring to these favorite ideas. Mrs. Shelley's note on *The Revolt of Islam* supplies us at this point with an extract too relevant to be ignored on the ground of its familiarity:

His inclinations led him (he fancied) almost alike to poetry and metaphysical discussions. I say "he fancied" because I believe the former to have been paramount, and that it would have gained the mastery even had he struggled against it. However, he said that he deliberated at one time whether he should dedicate himself to poetry or metaphysics.

It can hardly be doubted that this leaning to metaphysics was confirmed, if it was not partly occasioned,

---

[26] *Prometheus Unbound,* I. 440–42.

MATTER IN TERMS OF MIND 55

by that peculiar energy with which all objects that were powerful, weighty, and indefinite appealed to his sensitive imagination.[27]

[27] I have spoken of the presentation of matter in terms of mind as rare. In one way the common, almost vulgar, personification of rocks, streams, and the like may be comprised under this head, since they liken a material object to the spiritual side of human nature. The difference between these images and those cited above from Shelley is, I think, too obvious to require exposition.

Mixture of Matter and Spirit

THE ABOVE heading stands for a practice quite distinct in essence from the ordinary mixture of metaphors with which it is not seldom combined. Shelley, like most men who use figures freely and loosely, was subject to the last-named fault, a certain fluidity of nature which helped to make him, among other things, almost the foremost of English lyrists, enabling him to pass from one image to another with abnormal facility and swiftness. But the point we are now to discuss is of a subtler, rarer, and more interesting nature. The boundary between mind and matter, which is so clear and sharp to most minds, seems in many cases to have been very indistinct to Shelley. He passed from one state to the other with a rapidity which sometimes left him uncertain as to the side of the partition on which at a particular moment he chanced to be, or even, perhaps, skeptical as to the existence of a partition. Matter and mind approached each other, took on each other's properties, in his understanding the difference between them being hardly more marked than that between melting ice and congealing water. I proceed to give and explain some illustrations.

In the long simile from the third act of *The Cenci* quoted in the previous section [1] there are two parts, the

[1] *The Cenci*, III. i. 247–57.

MIXTURE OF MATTER AND SPIRIT

description of the material fact, the rock, and the description of its moral counterpart, the despairing soul. These two descriptions ought to be mutually exclusive, each confining itself to its own field of mind or matter. But Shelley cannot keep the moral element out of his picture of the rock; it sustains itself with "terror": and he cannot keep the material element out of his description of the soul; it

> Clings to the mass of life; yet clinging, leans,
> And leaning, makes more dark the dread abyss

It is a marriage between hermaphrodites.

Too much stress should not be laid on such interesting phrases as "green strength, azure hope, and eternity"[2] applied by a bold but not unexampled figure to the ivy, violet, and pine.[3] More significant is a passage like this:

> Death, Fear,
> Love, Beauty, are mixed in the atmosphere,[4]

Or observe the peculiar difficulty, the wrench, so to speak, with which the moral and material elements in the following are riven asunder, if we insist on an analysis of the passage:

> Ascend beside me, veilèd in the light
> Of the desire which makes thee one with me,[5]

---

[2] *An Ode: To the Assertors of Liberty*, 33.
[3] In the lovely lines
> The loud deep calls me home even now to feed it
> With azure calm out of the emerald urns

the calm is material and does not bear on the present point.
[4] *A Vision of the Sea*, 161-62.   [5] *Prometheus Unbound*, III. i. 34-35.

Is the veil here spiritual? Is the light spiritual? Strictly yes, because the veil is woven of the light and the light is moulded of the desire, which is an immaterial object. But do we conceive it in this way? Did Shelley so conceive it? Is not the picture called up that of a corporeal woman hidden from the bodily eye by a veil of material splendor? In other words, did not Shelley in the first place conceive of the light as moral, the light of desire, and afterwards as physical, enveloping and concealing not a mind but a body? No doubt a consistent metaphysical interpretation can be worked out, but would it represent the real thought of Shelley?

Here is a similar passage from the same scene:

> And, like a cloud, mine enemy above
> Darkens my fall with victory! [6]

Now that the shadow of an enemy should involve a falling antagonist in material darkness, that the victory of that enemy should darken the mind or the spirit of the vanquished, and that one of these facts should serve as the poetical symbol of the other is all perfectly natural and proper. But Shelley has perplexed the matter by his phraseology. The enemy darkens the fall, not with his advanced or projecting body, but with victory; that is, the *moral* cause is productive of the *physical* effect. I believe this confusion or coalescence could hardly arise in the mind of a man in whom the frontiers of the opposing kingdoms of mind and matter were definitely marked.

[6] *Ibid.*, III. i. 82–83.

MIXTURE OF MATTER AND SPIRIT

> Liberty
> From heart to heart, from tower to tower, o'er Spain
> . . . .
> Gleamed.[7]

Here is another curious passage. The gleam that passes from heart to heart is moral: hearts do not gleam in a physical sense, with the possible exception of that noblest of all hearts which lay unconsumed among the flames of the incinerating fire of Via Reggio. The gleam that passes from tower to tower is a physical gleam: the tower is undoubtedly a Spanish fortress, and to connect a spiritual gleam with a substantial fortress would be as absurd as to hang a metaphorical lamp from a literal ceiling, or to harness an actual horse to a figurative chariot. But Shelley identifies these two gleams with the sublime hardihood of one to whom the difference between inward and outward was not worth the trouble of a critical analysis.

> Athens diviner yet
> Gleamed with its crest of columns, on the will
> Of man, as on a mount of diamond, set [8]

This, at first sight, wears an aspect of extreme plausibility, since a mount of diamond forms a perfectly natural and fitting support for a crest of columns, but when we reflect that the figurative mount of diamond supports a literal crest of columns we are struck with the incongruity; the metaphor, in Shelley's plastic mind, had become a fact.

[7] *Ode to Liberty*, i. 2–5.   [8] *Ibid.* v. 9–11.

Love is almost material in some of Shelley's conceptions. Observe the curious juxtaposition with material things in the following:

> Some Spirit . . .
> . . . .
> . . . . passes with the warmth of flame,
> With love and odour and deep melody
> Through me, through me! [9]

> Be it love, light, harmony,
> Odour, or the soul of all
> Which from heaven like dew doth fall,
> Or the mind which feeds this verse
> Peopling the lone universe.[10]

There are here two groups of objects, one material (light, harmony, odor) and one immaterial (soul, mind); the singularity is that love is associated with the former group.

These points are interesting, but prove little. I proceed to less disputable evidence.

> Then by strange art she kneaded fire and snow
> Together, tempering the repugnant mass
> With liquid love — [11]

This reminds one a little of W. K. Clifford's famous simile of the train of cars held together by the sentiments of friendship between the stoker and the guard. The following is similar:

> and a light
> Of liquid tenderness, like love, did rise

---

[9] *Prometheus Unbound,* IV. 327–31.   [10] *Euganean Hills,* 315–19.
[11] *The Witch of Atlas,* xxxv. 1–3.

MIXTURE OF MATTER AND SPIRIT

> From her whole frame, an atmosphere which quite
> Arrayed her in its beams, tremulous and soft and bright [12]

Most of this is quite normal; it is quite permissible to a poet to speak of a light of tenderness emanating from the person of his heroine, and if he chooses to call this tenderness liquid, that is, I take it, free to shift and flow, he will offend only the finical. The dubious point, and the peculiarly Shelleyan point, is the simile, "like love." Why "like love," when we are expressly told that the light itself is only a metaphor of tenderness? The truth is, I believe, that when Shelley thought of love in the context, he thought of it as a highly delicate, mobile, atmospheric or liquid matter. Bearing this in mind, the comparison of this light of tenderness to such an aerial envelope becomes, if not justifiable from the everyday standpoint, intelligible, at least from the standpoint of Shelley.

But love is not always thought of as a liquid; it is also conceived as material warmth and fire.

> This is my torch-bearer
> Who let his lamp out in old time with gazing
> On eyes from which he kindled it anew
> With love [13]

By poetical standards, this is unexceptionable down to the end of the third line. A torch-bearer, in elfdom or nymphdom, may very well let his lamp go out in gaz-

---
[12] *The Revolt of Islam*, XI. v. 6–9.
[13] *Prometheus Unbound*, III. iii. 148–51; Shelley adds, "which is as fire, sweet daughter mine, For such is that within thine own." I omit these words in the text, since they complicate the matter, without, so far as I can see, affecting any point.

ing upon a pair of beautiful eyes; and the poets and lovers of all ages will justify him in relighting his torch at the eyes of his goddess. But with what should he relight it? Surely since the torch is material and likewise the eyes and their luster, he should rekindle it with their brightness. This will not do for Shelley. The material must be relighted at a moral, an immaterial, fire, the fire of love. I am less disposed to criticize the propriety of these combinations, though I think them liable to just criticism, than to point out the significance of the fact that their impropriety was imperceptible, or, at least, undisturbing, to Shelley. Love was to him so much of a real fire that it might serve as well to light a material torch as a figurative one.

> Whether that lady's gentle mind,
> No longer with the form combined
> Which scattered love, as stars do light,
> Found sadness where it left delight,[14]

The following is capable of two interpretations, only one of which is a support to our theory; it is the Moon, who addresses the Earth:

> Gazing on thee I feel, I know
> Green stalks burst forth, and bright flowers grow
> And living shapes upon my bosom move:
> Music in the sea and air,
> Wingèd clouds soar here and there,
> Dark with the rain new buds are dreaming of:
> 'Tis love, all love! [15]

[14] *The Sensitive Plant*, Conclusion, 5-8.
[15] *Prometheus Unbound*, IV. 363-69.

MIXTURE OF MATTER AND SPIRIT

In the ensuing passage it is very difficult to find any interpretation which will obviate the necessity of viewing both the illumination and the love which is its source as material:
> love, like the atmosphere
> Of the sun's fire filling the living world,
> Burst from thee, and illumined earth and heaven
> And the deep ocean and the sunless caves
> And all that dwells within them; [16]

In the citation which follows, there is, it seems to me, no escape from the admission that Shelley here conceives love as a physical emanation:
> overpowering light
> Of that immortal shape was shadowed o'er
> By love; which, from his soft and flowing limbs,
> And passion-parted lips, and keen, faint eyes,
> Steamed forth like vaporous fire; an atmosphere
> Which wrapped me in its all-dissolving power,[17]

I pass to a few other illustrations.
> And mouldering as they sleep, a thrilling sound
> Half sense, half thought, among the darkness stirs [18]

> sweet
> And subtile mists of sense and thought [19]

> For the spirit of life o'er every limb
> Lingered, a mist of sense and thought.[20]

In the following remarkable passage agony is described as having certain shadowy emanations, which

[16] *Ibid.*, II. v. 26–30.　　[17] *Ibid.*, II. i. 71–76.
[18] *A Summer Evening Churchyard*, 20–21.　[19] *Rosalind and Helen*, 808–09.
[20] *Ibid.*, 1013–14.

determine the form of the otherwise shapeless Furies, who assault and torture the sufferer:
> So from our victim's destined agony
> The shade which is our form invests us round;
> Else we are shapeless as our mother Night.[21]

That Shelley was an idealist in the Berkeleyan sense I shall try in a later section to prove or, at least, to support by cogent evidence. But I do not think that the mental habit which has been just now exemplified can be accounted for by any theoretic view of the illusoriness or unreality of matter. It is quite possible to regard matter as a form or phase of mind, and yet to preserve in unimpaired clearness the distinction between matter and the more normal and accredited forms of mind. An idealist may believe that an apple is nothing but a thought, and yet may be quite clear as to the fact that the apple in his orchard is applicable to certain ends of eating, selling, pickling, or cider-making which are quite out of the question with respect to the apple in his mind. He may be equally discriminating in his literary treatment of apples. I do not remember that Coleridge or Emerson is addicted to the habit just noted in Shelley. It is certainly true that materialism, the antipodal view, results in no blurring of the lines of demarcation between material and moral phenomena. The habit was an outgrowth of Shelley's temperament and would have survived a conversion to the doctrines of Holbach or Helvetius.

[21] *Prometheus Unbound*, I. 470–72.

MIXTURE OF MATTER AND SPIRIT

The bearing of this trait of Shelley's on our general subject is indirect but substantial. Our object is to prove the extent of Shelley's interest in mind, and the means employed has been the demonstration of his tendency to associate mind with matter, even where the results of that association were illogical and confusing.

Sleep

SLEEP BELONGS to that class of facts, so often instanced in this essay, which unite great force in the appeal to the imagination with a want of distinctness or definition in the appeal to the senses or the understanding. A sleeping man or animal may be definite enough, but the sleep-notion itself is among the most elusive, as it is among the most fascinating, of the conceptions with which nature has supplied us. The peace of sleep, its apparent comfort, its touching dependence and helplessness, the respite which it gives to care, sorrow, and even wickedness, the relegation of one form of consciousness and the entrance into another, the mystery and fantasy of dreams with their tradition of prophetic virtues, the restoration of bodily and spiritual energy which is felt in the moment of its departure, its somber relationship with death, have made sleep a favorite subject for the contemplation and exposition of poets. It had every claim on the regard of Shelley, and the interest he felt in all its aspects was more than commensurate with these claims.

In the discussion of this theme, I reserve, so far as possible, the topic of dreams for a succeeding section.

Queen Mab begins with the well-known passage:

> How wonderful is Death,
> Death and his brother Sleep!
> One, pale as yonder waning moon
> With lips of lurid blue;

SLEEP

> The other, rosy as the morn
> When throned on ocean's wave
> It blushes o'er the world;
> Yet both so passing wonderful! [1]

What may, in a sense, be called Shelley's first word as a poet to the English people is a magnifying and glorifying of sleep. The subsequent poem is the account of a vision disclosed to the sleeping mind of the maiden, Ianthe. An important — indeed the pivotal — passage in *Alastor*[2] is concerned with an experience in sleep. In *The Revolt of Islam* the Serpent sleeps in the woman's breast,[3] the woman sleeps,[4] Cythna sleeps,[5] Laon sleeps,[6] Laon sleeps again,[7] Laon sleeps in the last canto.[8] Sleep is often noted in *Rosalind and Helen*,[9] Cenci is slain in his sleep, and the rising of the curtain in the third scene of the last act of the drama finds Beatrice sleeping. In *Prometheus Unbound* much is made of the sleep of Panthea and Ione described in the second act,[10] and in the fourth act the curtain rises upon the sleep of Asia and Panthea. Sleep is rather conspicuous in *The Sensitive Plant* and holds a place of mark in *The Witch of Atlas*.[11] *Hellas* opens with the noble passage[12] descriptive of the sleep of Mahmud, in which the Indian invokes for her master a slumber which shall rival Heaven in clearness, brightness, and depth, and offers to renounce all her joys in exchange for the gift of an hour of quiet sleep to the ill-starred sultan.

[1] i. 1–8. [2] Lines 140–91. [3] I. xx. [4] I. xl.
[5] II. xxvii–xxviii. [6] III. i–vi. [7] III. xxii–xxiv. [8] XII. xvii–xviii.
[9] Lines 829–39. [10] II. i. 35–162. [11] Stanzas lx–lxxvi. [12] Lines 1–26.

The showing in passages of this kind is significant; but no one can form any idea of the extent to which Shelley's mind was dominated and fascinated by this idea who has not made some study of the frequency of individual allusions. Here is a point at which we may avail ourselves of the aid of Mr. F. S. Ellis's careful and valuable *Concordance*. My count of the references to the noun "sleep" as cited in this work is 202; of the references to the verb, including all uses of the word "sleeping," 153. Let us compare this with results obtainable from other poets. Tennyson was unusually prone to the introduction of sleep into his poetry, as the mere mention of the *Lotos-Eaters,* the *Day-Dream,* and the famous "Sleep, my little one" lyric will suggest. The only concordance to Tennyson to which I have access, that of Mr. Brightwell,* includes nothing much later than the first series of *Idylls;* even thus, the volume of poetry treated is equal, perhaps, to the entire poetical works of Shelley. In this concordance the noun "sleep" occurs 49 times to Shelley's 202; the verb "sleep" (in all forms) 88 times to Shelley's 153; noun and verb 137 times to Shelley's 355. According to Mr. Bradshaw's concordance Milton uses the noun "sleep" 33 times, the verb "sleep" 26 times. Shelley's total uses of the word in all forms are slightly in excess of Shakespeare's.

Nearly everything sleeps in Shelley. The earth:

The cold earth slept below.[13]

---

* At the time this was written, the Baker concordance had not been published. — *Ed.*

[13] *Lines,* "The cold earth slept below," 1.

SLEEP

The sea:
> Thou who didst waken from his summer dreams
> The blue Mediterranean, where he lay,
> . . . .
> And saw in sleep old palaces and towers [14]

The earth and ocean:
> The Earth and Ocean seem
> To sleep in one another's arms [15]

The moonlight:
> Where some old cavern hoar seems yet to keep
> The moonlight of the expired night asleep [16]
>
> The moon is veiled and sleeping now [17]

The sunset:
> When the sunset sleeps
> Upon its snow.[18]

The cloud:
> White clouds of noon which oft were sleeping [19]
>
> And all the night 'tis my pillow white
> While I sleep in the arms of the blast [20]

The waves:
> The whispering waves were half asleep [21]

The rivers:
> And at night they [Arethusa and Alpheus] sleep
> In the rocking deep
> Beneath the Ortygian shore [22]

---

[14] *Ode to the West Wind*, iii. 1–5. [15] *Epipsychidion*, 509–10.
[16] *Ibid.*, 553–54. [17] *Rosalind and Helen*, 141.
[18] *Prometheus Unbound*, IV. 491–92. [19] *The Revolt of Islam*, VII. xv. 3.
[20] *The Cloud*, 15–16. [21] *To Jane: The Recollection*, 13. [22] *Arethusa*, v. 13–15.

The winds:
> the very winds,
> Danger's grim playmates, on that precipice
> Slept [23]

The trees:
> Now all the tree-tops lay asleep,
> Like green waves on the sea [24]

> The woods were in their winter sleep,
> Rocked in that repose divine
> On the wind-swept Apennine; [25]

A few lines farther on a tree dies in sleep. The flowers:
> By the odour-breathing sleep
> Of faint night flowers [26]

Sleep is used of the passions as in the highly imaginative second line of the following:

> Kindness to such is keen reproach, which breaks
> With bitter stings the light sleep of Revenge [27]

Sleep is presented under impressive imagery. "Liquid sleep" is about as congenial to Shelley as "liquid love." Sometimes the combinations are very curious.

> And as those married lights, which from the towers
> Of Heaven look forth and fold the wandering globe
> In liquid sleep and splendour, as a robe [28]

The Moon. The shadow of white death has past
From my path in heaven at last,
A clinging shroud of solid frost and sleep [29]

---

[23] *Alastor*, 607–09.
[24] *To Jane: The Recollection*, 29–30.
[25] *With a Guitar, to Jane*, 46–48.
[26] *Prometheus Unbound*, II. i. 182–83.
[27] *Ibid.*, I. 393–94.
[28] *Epipsychidion*, 355–57.
[29] *Prometheus Unbound*, IV. 424–26.

SLEEP

He speaks above of "odour-breathing sleep."[26] He talks of the "caves of divine sleep."[30] With characteristic daring he does not shrink from a phrase like "the ocean of my sleep."[31] The melody of an old air is called "softer than sleep."[32]

> Thy sweet child Sleep, the filmy-eyed,
> Murmured like a noon-tide bee [33]

is part of an invocation to night. In a beautiful line, he speaks of "the wide pathless desert of dim sleep."[34]

He has high views of the nature and properties of sleep.

> or do I lie
> In dream, and does the mightier world of sleep
> Spread far around and inaccessibly
> Its circles? [35]

> Some say that gleams of a remoter world
> Visit the soul in sleep,[36]

> down, down, like that sleep
> When the dreamer seems to be
> Weltering through eternity; [37]

He seems to have thought that both sleep and death were appointed to unveil the realities which are screened from us by the illusions of daily life.

> Death is the veil which those who live call life:
> They sleep, and it is lifted.[38]

> The day's veil fell from the world of sleep [39]

---

[30] *Epipsychidion*, 194–95. [31] *Ibid.*, 308. [32] *Rosalind and Helen*, 1099.
[33] *To Night*, iv. 3–4. [34] *Alastor*, 210. [35] *Mont Blanc*, 54–57.
[36] *Ibid.*, 49–50. [37] *Euganean Hills*, 16–18.
[38] *Prometheus Unbound*, III. iii. 113–14. [39] *The Sensitive Plant*, i. 101.

72 POWER AND ELUSIVENESS IN SHELLEY

> Lift not the painted veil which those who live
> Call Life; though unreal shapes be pictured there,
> And it but mimic all we would believe
> With colours idly spread,[40]

The first of the three above quotations presents an obscurity. I interpret the first line by reversing the order of subject and predicate. The veil which those who live call life, that is, life in the usual sense, is death, in other words is a nothing, an illusion, a vanity. When they sleep — in common parlance, die — the veil that obscures actualities is removed. The second quotation appears to imply that Shelley attributed a like property to sleep.

To illustrate the poet's notion of sleep as the universal privilege of nature, I will quote in concluding this section two love stanzas, far less often quoted than others of no greater beauty.

> The cloud-shadows of midnight possess their own repose,
>   For the weary winds are silent, or the moon is in the deep;
> Some respite to its turbulence unresting ocean knows;
>   Whatever moves, or toils, or grieves, hath its appointed sleep.
> Thou in the grave shalt rest — yet till the phantoms flee,
>   Which that house and heath and garden made dear to thee ere-while
> Thy remembrance, and repentance, and deep musings are not free
> From the music of two voices, and the light of one sweet smile.[41]

[40] *Sonnet*, "Lift not the painted veil," 1-4.   [41] *Stanzas.—April, 1814*, 17-24.

Dreams

A DREAM is a phase of sleep so distinct from sleep *per se* and so often separately mentioned by Shelley that it merits a section to itself. The combination of the powerful and the intangible which attracted Shelley so strongly is manifest in the case of dreams.

Queen Mab is a dream, or at least a vision. The revelation of love in the form of a veiled maiden, which is the center of the story in *Alastor,* takes place during the poet's sleep in Cashmire. Passing by the beautiful parable in the first canto of *The Revolt of Islam* as revelations whose nature as dreams is not expressly avowed, I find Laon dreaming in the third canto of union with Cythna, flight, pursuit, and attack from "foul and ghastly shapes."[1] In *The Cenci* the doomed Beatrice dreams of reunion in Paradise,[2] and Paradise rather than slumber is the name applied to the dreams of the symbolic Lady in *The Sensitive Plant*.[3] In the second act of *Prometheus Unbound* Panthea dreams, first that Prometheus, arrayed in glory and exhaling love, appears to her in her sleep and mingles his life and spirit with hers; and second that "the lightning-blasted almond tree" bursts into "flower-infolding buds," which, riddled by a gust of wind, disclose on their petals the

[1] III. i–vi. [2] V. iii. 9–10.
[3] ii. 16; cf. "one whose dreams are Paradise," *Hellas,* 226.

legend "Follow, follow." Asia, too, dreams that the clouds and the herbs and the eyes of Panthea are inscribed with the same quickening mandate.[4] In *Epipsychidion* dreams in the sense of hopes and aspirations are somewhat indefinitely associated with the visions of bodily slumber: at times, however, sleep is expressly predicated.[5] In *Adonais* the poetical fancies or ideas of Keats are personified under the name of dreams. The Witch of Atlas diverts herself by curious or mischievous suggestions to the minds of the sleepers whom she visits. A terrible dream of Mahmud disturbs the opening choruses of *Hellas* and he is recalled to his waking senses by the wonder-working might of Ahasuerus. *The Triumph of Life* is avowedly "a waking dream."[6] In the *Fragments of an Unfinished Drama* there is a dream of a star descending among plants, disclosing a child-like spirit, which drops melon seeds or the like into a vase with murmurs of unintelligible melody.[7] A dream of Mrs. Leigh Hunt is elaborately recounted in one of the minor poems under the heading, *Marianne's Dream*. *A Vision of the Sea* has every mark of being the record of a nightmare. The lovely poem of *The Question* is a dream of spring and flowers.

Shelley employs the noun "dream-dreams" about 213 times in his poetry; the verb "dream" in all its forms 78 times. According to the imperfect concordance before named, Tennyson uses the noun 102 times (less than half as often as Shelley) and the verb 63 times

[4] II. i. *passim*. [5] See lines 190–344.
[6] Line 42. [7] Lines 125–50.

DREAMS

(not quite as often). Milton uses "dream," noun and verb, in all forms 34 times in his verse; Shakespeare about 191 times. Shelley's total uses amount to 291 (100 more than Shakespeare's). His record in this point is probably unparalleled in literature.

Many things dream in Shelley: The heavens:

> *The Earth.* I spin beneath my pyramid of night,
> Which points into the heavens dreaming delight,[a]

The moon:

> When she upsprings from inter-lunar dreams.[9]

Midnight:

> At dreaming midnight [10]

The earth:

> Thine azure sister of the spring shall blow
> Her clarion o'er the dreaming earth [11]

The sea:

> Thou who didst waken from his summer dreams
> The blue Mediterranean,[12]

The earth and ocean:

> The earth and ocean seem
> To sleep in one another's arms, and dream
> Of waves, flowers, clouds, woods, rocks and all that we
> Read in their smiles, and call reality [13]

---

[a] *Prometheus Unbound*, IV. 444–45. This passage, which is so clear to Miss Scudder and Mr. Forman that it does not even occur to them that it might bother anybody else, troubles me. According to the accepted punctuation, it would seem that "dreaming" qualifies "heavens."
[9] *Prometheus Unbound*, IV. 209.   [10] *Ode to Liberty*, xi. 13.
[11] *Ode to the West Wind*, i. 9–10.   [12] *Ibid.*, iii. 1–2.
[13] *Epipsychidion*, 509–12.

The woods, aboundingly:
> The woods were in their winter sleep
> . . . .
> And dreaming, some of Autumn past,
> And some of Spring approaching fast,
> And some of April buds and showers,
> And some of songs in July bowers,
> And all of love [14]

The plants:
> each flower and herb on Earth's dark breast
> Rose from the dreams of its wintry rest [15]
>
> the dreams of the Sensitive Plant [16]

The flowers:
> the flowers did they waken or dream [17]

The leaves:
> I bear light shade for the leaves when laid
> In their noon-day dreams [18]

The buds:
> Dark with the rain new buds are dreaming of [19]

The animals:
> And the beasts and the birds and the insects were drowned
> In an ocean of dreams without a sound [20]

The butterflies:
> many an antenatal tomb
> Where butterflies dream of the life to come [21]

---

[14] *With a Guitar, to Jane*, 46–53.
[16] *Ibid.*, i. 109.
[18] *The Cloud*, 4–5.
[20] *The Sensitive Plant*, i. 102–03.
[15] *The Sensitive Plant*, i. 7–8.
[17] *Ibid.*, ii. 3.
[19] *Prometheus Unbound*, IV. 368.
[21] *Ibid.*, ii. 53–54.

DREAMS

The serpent:
> the serpent heard it flicker
> In sleep, and dreaming still, he crept afar [22]

Art:
> Art's deathless dreams [23]

Human beings and conscious beings of all kinds dream *ad libitum*. Even ghosts dream:
> Such as ghosts dream dwell in the lampless deep.[24]

Dreams are presented under various and vivid imagery. A dream in *Prometheus Unbound* has plumes of flame.[25] Another is thus energetically personified in the same poem:

> Its rude hair
> Roughens the wind that lifts it, its regard
> Is wild and quick, yet 'tis a thing of air
> For thro' its grey robe gleams the golden dew
> Whose stars the noon has quenched not.[26]

The astonishing brilliancy and definiteness of the forms bestowed by Shelley in certain stanzas of *Adonais* on these airy exhalations of the mind has been already noted and illustrated.[27] That he owed something to the classic and perhaps to the Chaucerian and Spenserian practice of animating and personifying dreams we may freely concede without therefore slackening our belief in the power and the inclination of his own unassisted fancy to originate such forms, had origi-

---
[22] *The Witch of Atlas*, xxx. 4–5.
[24] *Prometheus Unbound*, IV. 245.
[26] II. i. 127–31.
[23] *Ode to Liberty*, iv. 12.
[25] I. 726.
[27] See page 43.

nation been called for. Other figures are used: the "ocean of dreams," the counterpart of the "ocean of his sleep," has been already cited; dreams are likened to summer flies,[28] to wizard flocks,[29] to a fierce and beauteous beast.[30] "The soft waving wings of noonday dreams"[31] is borrowed, in substance, from Milton. A dream is charmingly compared to a pilot:

> or what sweet dream
> May pilot us through caverns strange and fair
> Of far and pathless passion.[32]

Life itself is an "unquiet dream."[33] The phrase "silver dream" is twice used:

> By solemn vision, and bright silver dream
> His infancy was nurtured;[34]

a reminiscence, no doubt, of Milton's "clear dream and solemn vision."

> I slept, and silver dreams did aye inspire
> My liquid sleep[35]

In general, Shelley associates dreams and the dream-world with:

I. Happiness. I have already cited three instances in which sleep or its visions were assimilated to Paradise. Again in *Alastor:*

> Conduct to thy mysterious Paradise,
> O Sleep

---

[28] *The Witch of Atlas*, vl. 4.
[29] *Ode to Liberty*, viii. 9.
[30] *The Revolt of Islam*, VII. xxv. 3.
[31] *Prometheus Unbound*, III. iii. 145.
[32] *The Revolt of Islam*, VI. xxix. 1-3.
[33] *Hymn to Intellectual Beauty*, iii. 12.
[34] *Alastor*, 67-68.
[35] *Rosalind and Helen*, 768-69.

DREAMS

>Conducts, O Sleep, to thy delightful realms;[36]

where dreams are probably the occasion of the delight.

>With the delight of a remembered dream.[37]

The darker aspects of dream, though by no means forgotten, are less often emphasized.

II. Solemnity and elevation:

>Enough from incommunicable dream,
>And twilight phantasms, and deep noonday thought,
>Has shone within me,[38]

>   led
>By love, or dream, or God, or mightier Death [39]

>Why fear and dream and death and birth
>Cast on the daylight of this earth
>Such gloom; [40]

>   the dreaming clay
>Was lifted by the thing that dreamed below
>As smoke by fire,[41]

III. Reality. Observe once more the line previously quoted from *The Sensitive Plant:*

>And the day's veil fell from the world of sleep.[42]

In *Hellas,* Ahasuerus, calling up the phantasm of Mahomet II, addresses Mahmud:

>   What thou seest
>Is but the ghost of thy forgotten dream;
>A dream itself, yet less, perhaps, than that
>Thou call'st reality.[43]

---

[36] Lines 211–12, 219.   [37] *Prometheus Unbound,* II. i. 36.   [38] *Alastor,* 39–41.
[39] *Ibid.,* 427–28.   [40] *Hymn to Intellectual Beauty,* ii. 8–10.
[41] *Epipsychidion,* 338–40.   [42] i. 101.   [43] Lines 841–44.

The topic of shadow would be seasonable at this point, Shakespeare having told us that "a dream itself is but a shadow," and Shelley himself having a great fondness for the Shakespearian phrase "shadow of a dream," which appears in *The Sensitive Plant*[44] and the *Ode to Heaven*,[45] and which in the more ornate forms, "the bright shadow of that lovely dream"[46] and "a shadow of some golden dream,"[47] reappears in *Alastor* and *Epipsychidion*. But it seems best to postpone the discussion of this topic to the general heading "Effluence."

[44] Conclusion, 12.
[45] Line 36.
[46] *Alastor*, 233.
[47] *Epipsychidion*, 116.

Unearthly Beings

SHELLEY would not have been Shelley had he not felt a keen interest in the supernatural. Only a part of this interest, however, possesses a direct bearing on our immediate topic. The unreality of supernatural beings has not prevented them, in many cases, from developing a precision and a definiteness which rivals that of their flesh-and-blood associates. This has been the case in a marked degree with the fauns, satyrs, and Cyclops of the Greek myths, with the trolls and gnomes and nisses of Scandinavian and Teutonic legend, with the fairies and witches of the medieval romance, and with the genii of the *Thousand and One Nights*. A fondness for such types is no proof of a predilection for the elusive or the indefinite. It is conspicuous in a poet of an imagination so tangible as that of Keats: it is even found in Scott and Longfellow. What is really significant of a love for the combination of the potent and the indefinite is a strong interest in the more formless and misty products of the myth-making fancy of the race; in the beings called ghosts, phantoms, apparitions, or, more generally, spirits.

Shelley cared much for both these types of the supernatural. It is worth while, perhaps, to suspend for an instant the prosecution of our main purpose to note one or two peculiarities in the distribution of his interest among the members of the well-defined category. His references to the *dii majores* of Greece, even in a poem like *Prometheus Unbound,* are relatively few; with the Greek Pantheon at his beck he constructs a mythology of his own. The word "siren" does not occur in his works. He introduces two emasculated or, I might better say, disembruted, fauns in the *Prometheus,* who recite some verses mild and sweet enough to be chanted by peris or children. He has no interest in Northern myth; he mentions gnomes only twice, goblins only once, trolls never. He is comparatively fond of maenads and of fairies, and has a marked taste for genii. It is hardly necessary to add that his Witch of Atlas is no witch but a fairy, and that his Queen Mab is no fairy but an impersonation of the moral and intellectual forces in the universe.

To return to our proper subject: Among the English words which are notable for the power of dim suggestiveness, the word "shape" is conspicuous. The reader may recall the effective use that is made of the chilling properties of this word in Milton's account of Death at the gate of Hell, and in Coleridge's picture of the flying phantom in the *Wanderings of Cain.* Meaning shape, it suggests shapelessness, and its dimness and its force make it full of attractions for Shelley:

> beyond their inmost depth
> I see a shade, a shape:[1]
>
> the aerial kisses
> Of shapes that haunt thought's wildernesses[2]

[1] *Prometheus Unbound,* II. i. 119–20.   [2] *Ibid.,* I. 741–42.

UNEARTHLY BEINGS

I see thin shapes within the mist [3]

And among mighty shapes which fled in wonder,
And among mightier shadows which pursued [4]

That planet-crested shape swept by on lightning-braided pinions [5]

The subject in the above line is love; and the introduction of the vague substantive "shape" among the brilliant and relatively precise ideas aroused by "planet-crested" and "lightning-braided" is peculiar and noteworthy.

                    a Shape
So sate within, as one whom years deform,
Beneath a dusky hood and double cape,
Crouching within the shadow of a tomb; [6]

A Shape all light, which with one hand did fling
Dew on the earth, as if she were the dawn [7]

Shelley is prone to the use of spirits. In *Prometheus Unbound* the Spirit of the Hour, and the by no means identical Spirits of the Hours, the spirits of the human mind (two sets, one conspicuous in the first, the other clearly marked in the fourth act), and the Spirits of the Earth and the Moon and Demogorgon play important parts. On a very rough and hurried calculation I should say that about one-fourth of the drama was uttered by this one group or genus of supernatural beings. The most exquisite lyrics are assigned to their mouths, as if

---
[3] *Ibid.*, II. iii. 50.   [4] *The Revolt of Islam*, VII. x. 6–7.
[5] *Prometheus Unbound*, I. 765.   [6] *The Triumph of Life*, 87–90.
[7] *Ibid.*, 352–53.

humanity were no fit medium for the conveyance of their divine beauty. In some cases, those of the Earth and the Moon, for instance, the forms allotted to these beings are detailed and specific, if by no means flawlessly distinct; quite as often, or more often, the form is undefined. Some of them dwell

> Under pink blossoms or within the bells
> Of meadow flowers or folded violets deep,
> Or on their dying odours, when they die,
> Or in the sunlight of the spherèd dew? [8]

Allusions to spirits are frequent elsewhere. I select a number taken from a group of consecutive poems, many of them of great note, which fill only twenty-eight pages in Mr. Forman's eight-volume edition of Shelley's works.

The *Ode to Heaven* consists entirely of a chorus sung in strophes by three spirits. The West Wind is addressed as

> Wild Spirit, which art moving everywhere:
> Destroyer and preserver: hear, O, hear! [9]

and again in the last stanza the same invocation is employed:

> Be thou, spirit fierce,
> My spirit! [10]

In *The Cloud* we have the following:

> Wherever he dream, under mountain or stream,
> The Spirit he loves remains [11]

---
[8] *Prometheus Unbound*, II. ii. 84–87.   [9] *Ode to the West Wind*, i. 13–14.
[10] *Ibid.*, v. 4–5.   [11] Lines 27–28.

UNEARTHLY BEINGS

What the above "Spirit" is Shelley has not specified, and the commentators have imitated his reticence. It is probably the Spirit of water. *To a Skylark* begins

> Hail to thee, blithe spirit!
> Bird thou never wert [12]

And below:

> Teach us, sprite or bird,
> What sweet thoughts are thine.[13]

In the *Ode to Liberty* we have at the outset:

> Till from its station in the heaven of fame
> The Spirit's whirlwind rapt it [14]

At the close of the ode:

> The spirit of that mighty singing
> To its abyss was suddenly withdrawn [15]

Further examples are superfluous, but one may barely refer to the allegory of the *Two Spirits,* another dialogue between spiritual interlocutors.

Ghosts likewise have their meed of attention. His boyish feeling for them is recorded in lines of lofty restraint in the *Hymn to Intellectual Beauty:*

> While yet a boy I sought for ghosts, and sped
> Through many a listening chamber, cave and ruin,
> And starlight wood, with fearful steps pursuing
> Hopes of high talk with the departed dead.[16]

He speaks of ghosts tenderly:

[12] Compare Wordsworth's
  O Cuckoo! Shall I call thee bird,
  Or but a wandering voice?
[13] *To a Skylark,* 61–62.　　[14] i. 10–11.
[15] xix. 1–2.　　[16] v. 1–4.

> And gentle ghosts, with eyes as fair
> As star-beams among twilight trees [17]

"Mild and gentle ghost" [18] is the term applied to the spirit of Christ.

But the classical idea which associates these forms with multitude, forlornness, and desolation is also present to his fancy. Twice he finds in them a simile for the troops of dead leaves.

> And the leaves, brown, yellow, and gray, and red,
> And white with the whiteness of what is dead,
> Like troops of ghosts on the dry wind passed; [19]

And in the same vein, but with the addition of majesty to pathos,

> O wild West Wind, thou breath of Autumn's being,
> Thou, from whose unseen presence the leaves dead
> Are driven, like ghosts from an enchanter fleeing,
> Yellow, and black, and pale, and hectic red, [20]

Dante has used the opposite form of the simile,[21] as Longfellow has pointed out in his notes to the *Divine Comedy.*

But Shelley can pass from the classical conception, which is rather dreary than awful, to the full horror of the dim soul-curdling Teutonic idea. Beatrice describing the incipient plan of murder says:

> I whose thought
> Is like a ghost shrouded and folded up
> In its own formless horror [22]

[17] *To Coleridge,* 3-4.
[18] *Prometheus Unbound,* I. 554.
[19] *The Sensitive Plant,* iii. 34-36.
[20] *Ode to the West Wind,* i. 1-4.
[21] *Inferno,* iii. 112-17.
[22] *The Cenci,* III. i. 109-11.

In the mighty passage just quoted, Shelley's thought, like that of Beatrice, is shrouded and folded up in its own formless horror; the image cannot be exposed, tested, analyzed, but its magnificence is beyond question; it reduces to a sort of childishness the attempts of Poe, Bulwer, and others to exploit the ghost in terror-breeding narrative.

Compare the pure beauty of the following:

> The golden Day, which, on eternal wings,
> Even as a ghost abandoning a bier,
> Had left the Earth a corpse;[23]

Or the solemn pomp of the lines descriptive of the memory of Napoleon:

> He, by the past, pursued,
> Rests with those dead but unforgotten hours,
> Whose ghosts scare victor kings in their ancestral towers[24]

Phantoms or phantasms are also common in Shelley. On two distinct occasions they participate in the action. Prometheus wishes to hear the curse which he formerly pronounced against Jupiter and by a device which seems extravagant in the midst even of a drama in which extravagance is the plan and custom, the umbra or spectrum of Jupiter himself is called up to repeat the curse in lines whose passion and energy make us forgive, or forget, the grotesqueness of the device for their insertion. In *Hellas,* where the other phantom speaker appears, the reverse of this takes place; the contrivance is magnificent, but the execution, though apt, is unexcit-

---

[23] *Adonais,* xxiii. 3–5.   [24] *Ode to Liberty,* xii. 13–15.

ing. Nothing can be more picturesquely or dramatically contrived than the evocation of the ghost of the founder of an empire to utter the last words of menace and prophecy to the descendant from whose feeble grasp the scepter of the decaying line is gradually slipping. Demogorgon, also, whose pseudonym is Eternity, may be reckoned among the phantasms. Shelley has his Hades or Tartarus, dwelt upon in both *Hellas* and *Prometheus Unbound,* the seat of obscure powers and mystic lordships, of whom Demogorgon, another legacy perhaps from Milton, seems to be the chief.

> all the gods
> Are there, and all the powers of nameless worlds,
> Vast, sceptred phantoms; heroes, men, and beasts;
> And Demogorgon, a tremendous gloom [25]

Later on he is called a "mighty darkness." [26]

Other instances of the word "phantom," important here because indicative of a step farther into the inane and the inscrutable than the words "spirit" and "ghost," might be readily cited, but any doubts as to the reality of Shelley's interest in these and similar forms must be already dissipated.

[25] *Prometheus Unbound*, I. 204–07.   [26] *Ibid.*, II. iv. 2.

Landscape

LANDSCAPE may conveniently, though inaccurately, be taken to include all aspects of outward nature, sea, air, and light, as well as earth and vegetation. Everyone knows that there are degrees of precision and tangibility in the forms of eternal nature, that a stone is more definite or, at any rate, less mysterious, than a plant, a plant more definite than a dewdrop, a dewdrop more definite than a ray of light or breath of air. Now it will be found that, in a broad survey, the more definite a natural object is, the less Shelley cares for it; and every step in the direction of rarefaction or subtilization is a step toward the conquest of the affections of Shelley.

There are, of course, exceptions to the rule. The beauty of flowers, which must be counted among definite objects, secures a place for them in his heart; though even here I must note his peculiar interest in the most elusive of their properties, their fragrance, and the way he has when forced, so to speak, into a corner and obliged to describe them in some detail, of personifying and poeticizing them, turning them into Arcturi or maenads or naiads, or imitators of Narcissus, or children of the earth, or of the Hours. His feeling for trees seems strong, until we begin to compare it with his feeling for winds and clouds, when it recedes into insignificance. He is interested in birds, but chiefly in two kinds, birds of prey, by whom, as the attendants and symbols of victors and tyrants, his imagination was perennially excited, and songbirds, with whose music he is so engrossed that in the famous *To a Skylark* he makes the bird invisible. And in the two most elaborate descriptions of the nightingale which I recall,[1] there is no trait, unless "music-panting bosom" be reckoned as such, which appeals to any other sense than that of hearing. His feeling for mountains is less disputable; in fact, there can be no doubt that precision is no bar to his appreciation of the great and rugged. A review of the exceptions, however, leaves us scarcely less impressed than before with the extent of that partiality for the powerful and the elusive which is on the whole so rarely crossed or outweighed by other motives.

The impression thus aroused will be strengthened if we compare Shelley's interest in such positive subjects as form and color with his delight in the less substantial material conveyed in the shape of light or sound or odor. Form is among the most precise and the least impalpable of the appeals of outward nature to the aesthetic sense. Shelley is accordingly incapable of any keen or wide interest in form. A very few strikingly beautiful shapes attached to objects which are themselves markedly attractive, the prow of a boat or the curve of the young moon, appear and reappear in his compositions. But his habit on this point is silence. Color is very distinct in many cases, and Shelley,

[1] *Prometheus Unbound*, II. ii. 24–40; *Rosalind and Helen*, 1104–30.

though keenly alive to color, is not more sensitive to it than Scott or Keats or Coleridge or Tennyson, than almost any great modern poet with a taste for landscape is certain to be. When it comes to the elusive topics of light and sound and odor, his interest rises to heights which astonish even the students of his contemporaries. These tendencies will be illustrated in the sequel (Pages 110–30).

Wind

THE MOST intangible of all objects which are forms of matter, not modes of motion, is probably air or wind, and Shelley's delight in this phase of nature is vivid and insatiable. Let me offer at the outset one clear proof of the degree to which it occupied his thoughts.

A Defence of Poetry is not a treatise on wind, nor is it an essay on landscape: it is a logical or at least argumentative presentation of an abstract literary subject. It is no very long essay, occupying, in Mr. Forman's edition, about forty-six pages. It contains, nevertheless, five comparisons drawn from wind:

Man is an instrument over which a series of external and internal impressions are driven, like the alternations of an ever-changing wind over an Aeolian lyre.[1]

the poetry of the preceding age was as a meadow-gale of June [2]

Listen to the music, unheard by outward ears, which is as a ceaseless and invisible wind, nourishing its everlasting course with strength and swiftness.[3]

the mind in creation is as a fading coal, which some invisible influence, like an inconstant wind, awakens to transitory brightness: [4]

its footsteps are like those of a wind over the sea, which the morning calm erases.[5]

[1] *A Defence of Poetry*, p. 100.   [2] *Ibid.*, p. 118.   [3] *Ibid.*, p. 123.
[4] *Ibid.*, p. 137.   [5] *Ibid.*, p. 138.

Among the properties of wind which endeared it to Shelley are: (1) its invisibility, which appealed to his rarefied imagination; (2) the tender and caressing quality of its gentler movements, a type of the love he felt and sought; (3) its power of interpenetration with other substances, with sunlight, moisture, or cloud; (4) its office as purveyor or charioteer of various objects dear to Shelley: water, the clouds, the dead leaves, the winged seeds, sounds, and perfumes; (5) its office in the propulsion of boats: Shelley's passion for boats is well known; (6) its effects crisping the surface of the seas, lakes, fields, and the like; and (7) its use as a symbol for religious or poetical inspiration.

Much as he loves wind, he is fond, also, of the unmoved air:

> The lightest wind was in the nest [6]
>
> windless clouds o'er a tender sky [7]
>
> the windless sky [8]
>
> Be it bright as all between
> Cloudless skies and windless streams,
> Silent, liquid, and serene; [9]
>
> the windless heaven of June [10]
>
> the trances of the summer air [11]

The effect of absolute quiescence in *To Jane: The Recollection*, the poem from which the first of the above

---

[6] *To Jane: The Recollection*, 11.
[7] *The Sensitive Plant*, i. 97.
[8] *Rosalind and Helen*, 1106.
[9] *Prometheus Unbound*, I. 680–82.
[10] *Epipsychidion*, 80.
[11] *The Sunset*, 6.

extracts is taken, is almost unmatched in literature. One of the prime graces of the "Elysian City" (Naples) is that it enchants to calm "the mutinous air and sea."

He is fond of fading or fitful winds.

> The fitful wind is heard to stir
> One solitary leaf on high [12]

> His cheek would change, as the noonday sea
> Which the dying breeze sweeps fitfully [13]

> His motions, like the winds, were free,
> Which bend the bright grass gracefully,
> Then fade away in circlets faint; [14]

> The winds are still, or the dry church-tower grass
> Knows not their gentle motions as they pass [15]

> the warm and fitful breezes shake
> The fresh green leaves of the hedge-row briar [16]

> The light winds which from unsustaining wings
> Shed the music of many murmurings [17]

> with as inconstant wing
> As summer winds that creep from flower to flower [18]

They bring dew, or carry odor.

> A Sensitive Plant in a garden grew,
> And the young winds fed it with silver dew [19]

In *Alastor* the winds are twice called odorous;[20] and elsewhere

> The sweetness seems to satiate the faint wind [21]

---

[12] *Rosalind and Helen*, 123–24. [13] *Ibid.*, 1017–18. [14] *Ibid.*, 795–97.
[15] *A Summer Evening Churchyard*, 11–12. [16] *Rosalind and Helen*, 959–60.
[17] *The Sensitive Plant*, i. 78–79. [18] *Hymn to Intellectual Beauty*, i. 3–4.
[19] *The Sensitive Plant*, i. 1–2. [20] Lines 308, 538. [21] *Epipsychidion*, 108.

WIND

>   the noon-tide plumes of summer winds
> Satiate with sweet flowers [22]

> Like a rose embowered
>   In its own green leaves,
> By warm winds deflowered,
>   Till the scent it gives
> Makes faint with too much sweet those heavy-wingèd
>   thieves.[23]

> Then gentle winds arose,
> With many a mingled close
> Of wild Aeolian sound and mountain odour keen; [24]

They are associated, in a fashion almost peculiar to Shelley, with the sunbeams.

> Bright are the regions of the air,
>   And among the winds and beams
> It were delight to wander there — [25]

> And the winds and sunbeams with their convex gleams
>   Build up the blue dome of air [26]

The association with clouds is perpetual:

> Thou on whose stream, 'mid the steep sky's commotion,
> Loose clouds like earth's decaying leaves are shed [27]

In a lovely and well-known passage the clouds are likened to

>   thick flocks along the mountains
> Shepherded by the slow unwilling wind [28]

With less, but nevertheless with fine, effect the same simile is employed in *Hellas:*

---

[22] *Prometheus Unbound*, II. i. 37–38. [23] *To a Skylark*, 51–55.
[24] *Ode to Naples*, 23–25. [25] *The Two Spirits*, 5–7. [26] *The Cloud*, 79–80
[27] *Ode to the West Wind*. ii. 1–2. [28] *Prometheus Unbound*, II. i. 146–47.

> At length the battle slept, but the Sirocco
> Awoke, and drove his flock of thunderclouds
> Over the sea-horizon,[29]

Also:

> Or whether clouds sail o'er the inverse deep,
> Piloted by the many-wandering blast [30]

Sometimes both the wind and cloud are figurative; in the following light is combined with them:

> There late was One within whose subtle being,
> As light and wind within some delicate cloud
> That fades amid the blue noon's burning sky,
> Genius and death contended.[31]

The undulations wrought by the wind in water or corn are noted:

> And level with the living winds which flow
> Like waves above the living waves below [32]

Or again with imaginative vigor:

> And all the winds wandering along the shore
> Undulate with the undulating tide [33]

The assonance struck the poet and was repeated in ennobled form in the *Letter to Maria Gisborne:*

> The ripe corn under the undulating air
> Undulates like an ocean [34]

The winds are mixed with music. Take as an instance this delicate line:

> Whilst all the winds with melody are ringing [35]

---

[29] Lines 630–32.　[30] *Letter to Maria Gisborne,* 261–62.
[31] *The Sunset,* 1–4.　[32] *Epipsychidion,* 517–18.
[33] *Ibid.,* 433–34.　[34] Lines 119–20.　[35] *Prometheus Unbound,* II. v. 77.

Shelley was less, but only less, fond than Coleridge of the music of the Aeolian harp. In *Queen Mab* he has already learned to love

>the unmeasured notes
>Of that strange lyre whose strings
>The genii of the breezes sweep;[36]

To strong winds, unless they rose to the force of a whirlwind or a hurricane, Shelley was rather less partial than to the milder and sweeter mutations of the air. It may be questioned, however, if his success in handling them was not greater. Many of his allusions to mild winds are of a casual, slight, or preoccupied character, and his partiality for ideas of faintness and satiation sometimes offends the taste of robust critics. We must not forget that what is regarded as the supreme effort of his lyric genius, the *Ode to the West Wind,* is devoted to the celebration of a wind which he calls "fierce." In *Alastor* he says:

>the very winds,
>Danger's grim playmates, on that precipice
>Slept, clasped in its embrace[37]

It is interesting to note that the figure of the playmate, here applied to the fierce winds, occurs again in one of the most exquisite lines in which Shelley has recorded his affection for winds of the gentler type:

>and that tall flower that wets
>. . . . .
>Its mother's face, with heaven-collected tears,
>When the low wind, its playmate's voice, it hears.[38]

[36] i. 51–53.   [37] Lines 607–09.   [38] *The Question,* 13–16.

As in *Epipsychidion* he speaks of the waves of mild wind, so in the *Euganean Hills* he talks of the "billows of the gale."[39] In fact, the assimilation of wind to water, evinced in the patronage of such phrases as "stream of wind," is habitual and characteristic in Shelley.

He can rise in imagination and sink in logic to the level of the splendid but only half-intelligible phrase, "thunder-zoned"[40] winds. In storms his power is altogether adequate, as may be seen by a reference to the storm scenes in *The Revolt of Islam*,[41] in the *West Wind*,[42] and in *Prometheus Unbound*,[43] in which last burst of insurpassable lyric Shelley, with his curious gift of annexing when he chose other men's powers to his own, unites the momentum of Byron with the robust wholesomeness of Scott.

Shelley's favorite form of strong wind is the whirlwind, to which he is greatly, all but inordinately, addicted. Prometheus speaks of:

> The genii of the storm, urging the rage
> Of whirlwind [44]

and somewhat further on in the same speech apostrophizes the

> swift Whirlwinds, who on poisèd wings
> Hung mute and moveless o'er yon hushed abyss [45]

A few lines lower down, the Whirlwinds are talking, uttering among other things the energetic words,

[39] Line 55.   [40] *Ode to Liberty*, v. 7.   [41] I. iii–vii.   [42] Stanza ii.
[43] I. 708–22.   [44] *Prometheus Unbound*, I. 42–43.   [45] *Ibid.*, I. 66–67.

"silence is as hell to us."[46] A little below we have "whirlwind-peopled mountains";[47] and a little further yet, "The sound is of whirlwind underground."[48] Thus within the first 231 lines of the poem there are five allusions to whirlwinds, counting as one the two speeches which they utter. The hurricane, though not slighted, holds a less commanding position in Shelley's cave of Aeolus. It is characteristic of his preference for the indefinite that the poet, in spite of the *Ode to the West Wind,* is not given to specifying the directions from which winds blow: Libeccio is named, and Sirocco, and the north in at least one place; but the compass is not sedulously noted. Cold winds are not much affected; but in one powerful line Shelley has shown his mastery of the whipcord in the whir of the north wind, making his line a thong by the skillful repetition of the "wi(whi)" sound:

For Winter came: the wind was his whip [49]

The figurative uses of wind are numerous; but part of them have been already exemplified under other heads, and the remainder are scarcely of sufficient importance to justify the prolongation of this section by citations.

[46] *Ibid.,* I. 106.
[47] *Ibid.,* I. 204.
[48] *Ibid.,* I. 231.
[49] *The Sensitive Plant,* iii. 86.

Cloud

A CLOUD, having a definite though fugitive shape and a well-marked though unstable color, is a more palpable object than a breath or breeze. Still, if compared with a mountain, valley, river, tree, or flower, or viewed in the light of its tenuity and its fragility, its emergence from the invisible and its retreat into the invisible again, its situation in the mysterious upper atmosphere, and its power to tantalize without quite satisfying the imagination, it must be reckoned among impalpable things. Up to our time, poetry has scarcely done it justice. The cloud of early periods is the rain or storm cloud, that is, the cloud that had a practical bearing on man's comfort or prosperity. So pervasive and persistent was this sense that even now cloud, in metaphor, means only trouble or depression. Later on the bright clouds come to be regarded, but at first only in the resplendence of their sunrise or sunset coloring. The white clouds of the full day, beautiful and conspicuous as they are, have been long slighted even by those whose poetical calling disposed, and even bound, them to be prompt in the welcome of their beauty. Shelley and Ruskin are perhaps the only two writers of modern English who have been duly susceptible to their splendor and significance. Shelley is as devoted to clouds as if he had set himself to the task of atoning in his single person for the apathy and neglect of all other poets. They seem never to have been long out of his mind. The persistence and frequency of his references to this topic amounts to a pronounced mannerism, that is, if we define mannerism as a literary habit pushed to eccentricity. If we associate affectation with the term, he had no mannerisms. Among the things which aided in the subjugation of his mind by this beautiful phase of nature were the following: (1) the aerial situation of clouds: the atmosphere had always a spell for Shelley; (2) their tenuity and evanescence; (3) the invisible state which is, to borrow a Shelleyan phrase, both their cradle and their grave; (4) their effective combination with many other noble objects of nature, the sky, the sun, the moon, the stars, the rain, the lightning, the thunder, the rainbow, and the mountain-peak; (5) their porosity, or penetrability, by wind or sunshine, their general relation to wind being also highly significant; (6) their mobility and prolonged journeys; (7) their effects on earth and man in the renewal of beauty in vegetation and the provision of food and water.

To cite miscellaneous instances in any practical or moderate number, say fifty, for example, would be as futile as it would be easy, because the number could probably be paralleled from other poets whose passion for clouds fell far short of that of Shelley. The frequency of references in a narrow compass, however, offers a more satisfactory proof. Take the poem *To a Skylark,* for example. This poem is on a bird, not a cloud, and the only direct connection with clouds is their possible presence in the skies in which the bird soars. In the eighth line, nevertheless, the skylark is likened to "a cloud of fire." In lines 11 to 14 it is said to float and run among the brightening clouds that envelop the sunken sun in their golden lightning. In lines 28 to 30 we have the simile, in reference to the unseen bird's voice,

> As, when night is bare,
> From one lonely cloud
The moon rains out her beams, and heaven is overflowed.

In lines 33 to 35 we are told the drops from rainbow clouds are less bright than the rain of melody from the skylark. Here are four allusions in the space of thirty-five lines of a poem whose subject is a bird.

The Revolt of Islam contains a beautiful dedication to Mary Shelley. This dedication contains fourteen Spenserian stanzas, or a total of one hundred and twenty-six lines, it is not on the subject of clouds, and it contains only one brief landscape, in which clouds are not mentioned. It contains, however, three references:

The clouds which wrap this world from youth did pass [1]

> And walked as free as light the clouds among [2]

> Two tranquil stars while clouds are passing by [3]

In the fourth, fifth, and sixth stanzas of the first canto of *The Revolt of Islam* there are five allusions to clouds,

[1] *The Revolt of Islam*, iii. 2.   [2] *Ibid.*, vii. 6.   [3] *Ibid.*, xiv. 6.

but the showing is really less remarkable since the subject is a tempest. I cite three of these examples, however, as illustrative of Shelley's treatment and, in particular, of his love for white and for interwoven clouds, giving only references to the other passages.[4]

>   the blue sky was seen
> Fretted with many a fair cloud interwoven
>   Most delicately,[5]

>   the vast clouds fled,
> Countless and swift as leaves on autumn's tempest shed.[6]

>   blue light did pierce
> The woof of those white clouds, which seemed to lie
> Far, deep, and motionless;[7]

In *Hellas,* Hassan utters a speech of sixty-three lines descriptive of a sea-fight in which the word "cloud" occurs six times. The uses are all figurative and illustrate Shelley's constant resort to this unfailing storehouse of metaphor and simile:

> Four hundred thousand Moslems, from the limits
> Of utmost Asia, irresistibly
> Throng, like full clouds at the Sirocco's cry,[8]

> When the fierce shout of Allah-illa-Allah
> Rose like the war-cry of the northern wind,
> Which kills the sluggish clouds,[9]

> Like sulphurous clouds, half-shattered by the storm,
> They [the fleets] sweep the pale Aegean [10]

[4] *Ibid.,* I. vi. 2, 7.   [5] *Ibid.,* I. iv. 2–4.
[6] *Ibid.,* I. iv. 8–9.   [7] *Ibid.,* I. v. 3–5.
[8] *Hellas,* 275–77.   [9] *Ibid.,* 290–92.
[10] *Ibid.,* 302–03.

> Russia still hovers, as an eagle might
> Within a cloud, near which a kite and crane
> Hang tangled in inextricable fight,
> To stoop upon the victor; [11]
>
> Like clouds, and like the shadows of the clouds,
> Over the hills of Anatolia,
> Swift in wide troops the Tartar chivalry
> Sweep; [12]

In making the count I have not included

> lofty ships even now,
> Like vapours anchored to a mountain's edge,
> Freighted with fire and whirlwind, wait at Scala [13]

though the vapours here mentioned are probably nothing more than clouds. Mahmud's reply to Hassan has not reached the length of three lines before he says, in a noble phrase:

> Upon that shattered flag of fiery cloud
> Which leads the rear of the departing day [14]

Noble as the entire Hassan-Mahmud passage is,[15] it will be observed that the resemblance to clouds in most of the figures is not at all striking. Images drawn from clouds, like images seen in them, are likely to reveal a good deal of the uncertainty and indistinctness of the clouds themselves, and to follow Shelley in all his similes would require the flexibility of assent which Polonius gave to Hamlet's successive discovery of a whale, a weasel, and a camel in the cloud-shapes of the

---

[11] *Ibid.*, 307–10.   [12] *Ibid.*, 328–31.
[13] *Ibid.*, 283–85.   [14] *Ibid.*, 338–39.
[15] *Ibid.*, 273–346.

CLOUD

Danish heavens. Take the following passage, the beauty of which is scarcely marred by the imperfection of the alleged resemblance:

> The pyramids
> Of the tall cedar overarching, frame
> Most solemn domes within, and far below,
> Like clouds suspended in an emerald sky,
> The ash and the acacia floating hang
> Tremulous and pale [16]

It is interesting at this point to set down the fact that Shelley has at least four times compared himself to a cloud, two of these occurring among his noblest and most famous passages. I give the examples:

> I faint, I perish with my love! I grow
> Frail as a cloud [17]

> Secure o'er rocks and waves I weep
> Rejoicing like a cloud of morn [18]

> If I were a dead leaf thou mightest bear;
> If I were a swift cloud to fly with thee;
> . . . .
> Oh! lift me as a wave, a leaf, a cloud [19]

> 'Midst others of less note, came one frail Form,
> A phantom among men; companionless
> As the last cloud of an expiring storm
> Whose thunder is its knell; [20]

Compare the choice of the cloud as the symbol of solitude with the "lonely cloud" just quoted from the

---

[16] *Alastor*, 433–38. [17] *Two Fragments on Love*, i. 1–2.
[18] *To Constantia, Singing*, iv. 6–7. [19] *Ode to the West Wind*, iv. 1–2, 11.
[20] *Adonais*, xxxi. 1–4.

Skylark and with the first line of Wordsworth's *Daffodils,* "I wandered lonely as a cloud." Contrast it with Shelley's fondness for making the clouds *gregarious* in the most literal sense by likening them to flocks of sheep.[21] (See page 95.) We may add the lovely lines in *Prometheus Unbound,*

> Look, sister, where a troop of spirits gather,
> Like flocks of clouds in spring's delightful weather,
> Thronging in the blue air! [22]

The first semichorus in *Hellas* exclaims:

> Would I were the wingèd cloud
> Of a tempest swift and loud! [23]

In the fragment *A Cloud Chariot* Shelley says,

> O that a chariot of cloud were mine!
> Of cloud which the wild tempest weaves in air.[24]

I cannot refrain from quoting in full, partly as an instance of the mixture of the extremes of boldness and felicity in the matter of finding similes for clouds, but largely on the ample warrant of its unapproached and unutterable beauty, the second stanza of the *Ode to the West Wind.*

> Thou on whose stream, mid the steep sky's commotion,
> Loose clouds like earth's decaying leaves are shed,
> Shook from the tangled boughs of Heaven and Ocean,
>
> Angels of rain and lightning: there are spread
> On the blue surface of thine airy surge,
> Like the bright hair uplifted from the head

---

[21] Lowell has combined the ovine with the solitary conception: "Where one white cloud like a stray lamb doth move." *To the Dandelion.*
[22] I. 664-66.   [23] Lines 648-49.   [24] Lines 1-2.

Of some fierce Maenad, even from the dim verge
Of the horizon to the zenith's height,
The locks of the approaching storm. Thou dirge

Of the dying year, to which this closing night
Will be the dome of a vast sepulchre,
Vaulted with all thy congregated might

Of vapors, from whose solid atmosphere
Black rain, and fire, and hail will burst: oh hear!

In view of the vehement objection that has been made to Byron's comparison of the space-filling objects, Night and Storm and Darkness, to the diminutive eye of a woman, it is interesting to note that Shelley's comparison of the whole sky from horizon and zenith to a woman's hair has escaped criticism. To my mind the innocence of Shelley is more obvious than the guilt of Byron. The second simile, drawn from a sepulchral dome, is of that kind of excellence which makes silence the only refuge from the humiliating collapse of every effort at commensurate praise.

The interfusion of cloud and light, or cloud and wind, is especially fascinating to Shelley.

As the warm aether of the morning sun
Wraps ere it drinks some cloud of wandering dew [25]

As the radiant lines of morning
  Through the clouds ere they divide them; [26]

     From one lonely cloud
The moon rains out her beams [27]

[25] *Prometheus Unbound*, II. i. 77–78.   [26] *Ibid.*, II. v. 56–57.
[27] *To a Skylark*, 29–30.

>   whence is the light
> Which fills the cloud? . . .
> . . . .
>   . . . and the light
> Which fills this vapour, as the aerial hue
> Of fountain-gazing roses fills the water,[28]
>
> And bears me as a cloud is borne by its own wind.[29]
>
>   gathering like a cloud
> The very wind on which it rolls away [30]
>
> wind-enchanted shapes of wandering mist; [31]
>
> As light and wind within some delicate cloud.[32]

It is well known that among Shelley's lyrics one of the best and the only one perhaps of the number that can fairly be called popular is devoted to *The Cloud*. In the poem the first stanza deals with the beneficent offices of the cloud, the second with its terrors, the third, fourth, and fifth with the effects of its commixture with the great lights of the firmament, sunrise, sunset, the moon, the rainbow, and the fifth (with an undertone of faint suggestion of man's own death and immortality) with the dissolution and reappearance of the mobile and melting vapor in the heavens. The first person, employed throughout in the poem and never used elsewhere, as I recall, of any inanimate object,[33] is significant of the thoroughness and facility with which Shelley identified himself with this aerial and elusive

---

[28] *Prometheus Unbound*, II. v. 8–13.   [29] *Ibid.*, IV. 324.
[30] *The Revolt of Islam*, II. xxxi. 2–3.   [31] *Prometheus Unbound*, II. iii. 27.
[32] *The Sunset*, 2.   [33] The *Hymn of Apollo* is a very doubtful exception.

work of nature. How powerfully the cloud affected him may be divined from two lines of *Rosalind and Helen:*

> If but a cloud the sky o'ercast,
> You might see his colour come and go [34]

Compare this with the effect of the changes in the wind on the Lady of *The Sensitive Plant:*

> the coming and going of the wind
> Brought pleasure there and left passion behind [35]

[34] Lines 1019–20.   [35] ii. 23–24.

Light

I NEXT TAKE up the three correlated topics of light, sound, and odor, three things which combine potency and elusiveness with a hold of no ordinary force on the mind of Shelley. In listing the forms of light which enthralled his imagination I shall have listed all the chief natural sources of light in the known universe:

1. The sun: less loved, perhaps, than other luminaries, but still often and sympathetically mentioned, now in the Greek form of the "all-beholding Sun,"[1] now as

>   Broad, red, radiant, half-reclined
>   On the level quivering line
>   Of the waters crystalline;[2]

now with even more than wonted beauty combined with a much more than wonted exactness,

>   The white sun twinkling like the dawn
>   Out of a speckled cloud;[3]

now personified in the *Hymn of Apollo*.

2. The sunrise: chosen as the time of opening no fewer than three acts of *Prometheus Unbound;*[4] resplendent in the *Euganean Hills;* personified in a strangely drastic and poignant form in the magnificent "eagle" simile of *The Cloud.*[5]

---

[1] *Prometheus Unbound*, I. 26; *The Witch of Atlas*, ii. 2.
[2] *Euganean Hills*, 101–03. [3] *To Jane: The Recollection*, 67–68.
[4] I, II, IV. [5] Lines 31–38.

LIGHT

3. The sunset: relieving with momentary effulgence the long disquisitions of *Queen Mab;*[6] giving subject and title to a not uninteresting poem;[7] embosoming the flight of the skylark; timing the song of Laone in *The Revolt of Islam*[8] and the visit of the lonely seeker of Ahasuerus; enriching the opening passage of *Julian and Maddalo;*[9] now terrible as the "last glare of day's red agony" in the third act of *Prometheus Unbound;*[10] now tender as it sleeps upon the snow[11] in the last act of the same poem.

4. The moon: deeply cherished and constantly employed by Shelley; opening as the type of death the first section of *Queen Mab;*[12] the subject (and object) of one of the most powerful of his briefer lyrics;[13] appearing as a distinct and important character in the jubilant chants of the last act of *Prometheus Unbound;* used again and again and again as the symbol of tottering Islam in the lyrics and dialogues of *Hellas;* appearing as the "Mother of the Months" in *The Witch of Atlas;*[14] exquisitely personified in *The Cloud;*[15] applied three times to Emilia Viviani in different connections in the space of less than a hundred lines of *Epipsychidion;*[16] and serving three times as the index of the color of white flowers.[17]

5. The planet Venus: not less dear than the moon; figured as the symbol of liberty and love in the comet

[6] ii. 1-21. [7] *The Sunset.* [8] V. li. st. 1. [9] Lines 54-85.
[10] III. ii. 7. [11] IV. 491-92. [12] i. 3-4. [13] *To the Moon.*
[14] iv. 1. [15] Lines 45-52. [16] Lines 27, 81-82, 117-19.
[17] *The Sensitive Plant,* i. 34; *The Question,* iii. 2; iv. 6.

and morning star passage of *The Revolt of Islam;*[18] beautifully described in the *Epipsychidion* lines:

> Bright as that wandering Eden Lucifer,
> Washed by the soft blue Oceans of young air;[19]

and again referred to in the same poem where Emilia's splendor leaves "the third sphere pilotless";[20] invoked as the home of the spirit of love and beauty in the *Ode to Naples;*[21] furnishing Adonais with the proud title of "thou Vesper of our throng";[22] probably also figuring as the "star whose insolent and victorious light" triumphs over the falling moon of Islam;[23] again combined with the moon as the "white star, its sightless pilot's crest" of the floating bark of the light-laden moon;[24] or, in the *Euganean Hills,*[25] as the star that seems to minister to the moon half the crimson light she brings from the sunset; and supplying in *The Witch of Atlas* a pretext for Vulcan's building of the airy boat.[26]

6. The stars: "splendour-wingèd" in the *Epipsychidion;*[27] "a swarm of golden bees" in *The Cloud;*[28] reeling and dancing like fireflies;[29] scattering "drops of golden light" in a beautiful passage of the *Prometheus Unbound;*[30] furnishing beautiful epithets, "star-inwoven," "star-inwrought,"[31] to the mantles of the phantasm of Jupiter and of the spirit of the Night;

[18] I. xxvi. [19] Lines 459–60. [20] Line 117.
[21] Lines 149–55. [22] xlvi. 9. [23] *Hellas,* 337–47.
[24] *Prometheus Unbound,* III. ii. 26–28. [25] Lines 321–26.
[26] Stanza xxxi. [27] Line 81. [28] Line 54.
[29] *The Witch of Atlas,* xxviii. 5–6. [30] II. ii. 20.
[31] *Prometheus Unbound,* I. 234; *To Night,* ii. 2.

the object of the moth's desire;[32] or typifying the height of human aspiration, "The loftiest star of unascended heaven."[33]

7. The comet: less often named, but by no means forgotten; figuring as the baleful symbol in the morning-star-comet parable of *The Revolt of Islam*,[34] and probably representing Harriet Shelley in the *Epipsychidion* lines:

> Thou too, O Comet, beautiful and fierce,
> Who drew the heart of this frail Universe
> Towards thine own;[35]

8. The meteor: rivaled only, if rivaled at all, by the moon and the planet Venus in the strength and tenacity of its hold on Shelley's affection; lighting the bridal couch of Laon and Cythna;[36] rising out of the water-bubbles to be the vehicle of spirits;[37] becoming a transient form of *The Witch of Atlas*;[38] descending among plants and flowers and disclosing the form of a spirit-child;[39] supplying flags to armies of sprites;[40] signaling the consent of Ahasuerus;[41] picturing the movement of Ariel, "like a living meteor";[42] employed metaphorically as the type of happiness,[43] or of the mind of Coleridge: "A cloud-encircled meteor of the air."[44]

9. The lightning: the pilot of *The Cloud*;[45] appear-

---

[32] *To* ———, "One word is too often profaned," ii. 5.
[33] *Prometheus Unbound*, III. iv. 204.
[34] I. xxvi.
[35] Lines 368-70.
[36] *The Revolt of Islam*, VI. xxxii–xxxiv.
[37] *Prometheus Unbound*, II. ii. 70-82.
[38] iii. 5.
[39] *Fragments of an Unfinished Drama*, 126-50.
[40] *The Witch of Atlas*, stanza lii.
[41] *Hellas*, 175-77.
[42] *With a Guitar: To Jane*, 22.
[43] *Queen Mab*, iv. 101.
[44] *Letter to Maria Gisborne*, 207.
[45] Line 18.

ing in "momentary oceans" and in "dawn-tinted deluges of fire";[46] employing the cloud as its angel;[47] braided among the pinions of the "planet-crested" Love;[48] applied in metaphor in such phrases as "The lightning of the noontide ocean"[49] or "the golden lightning of the sunken sun."[50]

10. The firefly: one citation will suffice:

> Like wingèd stars, the fire-flies flash and glance,
> Pale in the open moonshine, but each one
> Under the dark trees seems a little sun,
> A meteor tamed, a fixed star gone astray
> From the silver regions of the milky way.[51]

11. The glow-worm: providing one of the many similes for the invisible skylark, "Like a glow-worm golden in a dell of dew";[52] furnishing a delicate allusion to "folded lilies in which glow-worms dwell"[53] or to flower-pavilions roofing glow-worms from the dew.[54]

As an illustration of the copiousness of Shelley's references to light, I will take the passage from the beginning of stanza xliv to the end of stanza li of *The Witch of Atlas*. In stanza xliv we have "stars of fire" in the second line, "Sun's dominions" in the third, "golden glow" in the fourth, and "moonlight splendour" in the seventh. In stanza xlv we have "like a star up the torrent of the night" in the fourth line, and "the morning

---

[46] *Hellas*, 959, 963. [47] *Ode to the West Wind*, ii. 4.
[48] *Prometheus Unbound*, I. 765.
[49] *Stanzas written in Dejection near Naples*, ii. 6.
[50] *To a Skylark*, 11–12. [51] *Letter to Maria Gisborne*, 281–85.
[52] *To a Skylark*, 46–47. [53] *The Witch of Atlas*, xxxix. 5.
[54] *The Sensitive Plant*, i. 55–57.

glare" in the fifth. In stanza xlvi we have "Like sunlight" in the first line, "noon-wandering meteor flung to Heaven" in the second, "radiant hair" in the fifth. In stanza xlvii we have "weary moon" in the first line, "noon of interlunar night" in the second, "the light of shooting stars" in the fourth and fifth. In stanza xlviii we have "Antarctic constellations" in the third line and "Canopus and his crew" in the fourth. In stanza xlix we have "translucent floor" in the first line and "tremulous stars" in the second. In stanza l we have "the lightning flash" in the fifth line. In stanza li we have a "shooting star" in the second line and "late moon" in the seventh.

After this, the reader who has not consulted the poem concludes, of course, that the subject of the passage is the heavens or some illumination. Nothing of the sort: there are two subjects, a supernatural hermaphrodite and a voyage in the southern hemisphere. The allusions to light are *obiter dicta*.

Some idea of Shelley's predilection for light may be derived from his combinations of different forms of light. Moon, sunset, and star are a favored combination.

> Autumn's evening meets me soon,
> Leading the infantine moon,
> And that one star, which to her
> Almost seems to minister
> Half the crimson light she brings
> From the sunset's radiant springs:[55]

[55] *Euganean Hills*, 321–26.

> The floating bark of the light-laden moon
> With that white star, its sightless pilot's crest,
> Borne down the rapid sunset's ebbing sea;[56]

Observe in the above quotations, the very positive and precise nature of the relations attributed to the form of light.

> And far o'er southern waves, immovably
> Belted Orion hangs — warm light is flowing
> From the young moon into the sunset's chasm.[57]

Those who wish to form a clear notion of Shelley's regard for light should read the conclusion of the first and the beginning of the second sections of *Queen Mab*,[58] the description of the cup-bearing shape in *The Triumph of Life;*[59] the *Lines written among the Euganean Hills;* the *Promethesus Unbound* throughout; and the *Epipsychidion*, particularly from line 276 to line 383.

We must not forget that it was Shelley who told us in a line which Wordsworth ought to have valued for its union of poetical force with the straightforwardness of bare prose: "Men scarcely know how beautiful fire is,"[60] adding in diction more characteristically his own:

> Each flame of it as a precious stone
> Dissolved in ever-moving light[61]

I have already quoted extensively from *The Witch of Atlas*, but I cannot refrain from noting that the stanza before the one just referred to contains the

---

[56] *Prometheus Unbound*, III. ii. 26–28.
[57] *Prince Athanase*, 196–98.
[58] i. 222–77; ii. 1–46.
[59] Lines 337–53.
[60] *The Witch of Atlas*, xxvii. 3.
[61] *Ibid.*, xxvii. 4–5.

phrase "sweet splendour"[62] and the original epithet "fountain-lighted";[63] that the following stanza is embellished with "green splendour"[64] and with a picture of reeling constellations;[65] and that the next stanza to that mentions "an inextinguishable well of crimson fire."[66] But one will have time to list the allusions to light in Shelley when one has leisure to count the stars.

[62] *Ibid.*, xxvi. 6. [63] *Ibid.*, xxvi. 3.
[64] *Ibid.*, xxviii. 4. [65] *Ibid.*, xxviii. 5.
[66] *Ibid.*, xxix. 6–7.

Sound

It may be questioned whether sound should have a place among elusive or indefinite phenomena. Sound, as language proves, is capable of minute subdivision and discrimination, and a sonata of Beethoven is a collection of units as precisely defined and as strongly marked, perhaps, as a bed of flowers or a set of diamonds. But sound, unlike sights, is fleeting; it cannot retain for the imagination the precision which it supplied, in the first instance, to the perceptions: it becomes indistinct through the incapacity of the memory to recall, to revise, and to confirm its impressions. A picture of Corot that is out of sight is a far more definite object to the mind than an overture of Wagner that is out of hearing. Moreover, the vanquishing of the sound itself, quite apart from its eclipse in the memory, gives it a mystical and unreal quality, a kinship with those elfin and ghostly beings which it imitates in the swiftness of its disappearance. It rides, as it were, on time, and the steed imparts its elusiveness to the rider. That we habitually resort to sight to quiet the fears that have been excited by sounds is a proof that sound belongs to a world which, compared with the province of sight, is unearthly and mystical.

I cite first as an example of the singular fullness and expansiveness of Shelley's representation of sound a passage from the second act of *Prometheus Unbound*.

SOUND

Semichorus II

There the voluptuous nightingales,
   Are awake through all the broad noonday:
When one with bliss or sadness fails,
   And through the windless ivy-boughs,
  Sick with sweet love, droops dying away
On its mate's music-panting bosom;
Another from the swinging blossom,
    Watching to catch the languid close
   Of the last strain, then lifts on high
   The wings of the weak melody,
Till some new strain of feeling bear
   The song, and all the woods are mute;
When there is heard through the dim air
The rush of wings, and rising there,
   Like many a lake-surrounded flute,
Sounds overflow the listener's brain
So sweet, that joy is almost pain.

Semichorus I

There those enchanted eddies play
   Of echoes, music-tongued, which draw,
   By Demogorgon's mighty law,
   With melting rapture, or sweet awe,
All spirits on that secret way,
   As inland boats are driven to Ocean
Down streams made strong with mountain-thaw;
And first there comes a gentle sound
To those in talk or slumber bound,
   And wakes the destined; soft emotion
Attracts, impels them; those who saw
Say from the breathing earth behind
There steams a plume-uplifting wind
Which drives them on their path, while they
   Believe their own swift wings and feet

>   The sweet desires within obey;
>   And so they float upon their way,
>   Until, still sweet, but loud and strong,
>   The storm of sound is driven along,
>   Sucked up and hurrying; as they fleet
>   Behind, its gathering billows meet
>   And to the fatal mountain bear
>   Like clouds amid the yielding air.[1]

The devotion of thirty-nine consecutive lines to the representation of sound is too rare in literature not to be highly significant. Compare with this the long passage at the end of Act II,[2] in which Asia describes sound not only at equal length but by the aid of precisely the same figure, that of moving and rushing water. The kinship of sound and water was an inexhaustible stimulus to Shelley. The "sea profound, of ever-spreading sound"[3] may be compared with the "ocean of splendour and harmony"[4] in the fourth act, with "the clear billows of sweet sound"[5] in the second act, and with the most striking, perhaps, of all the examples of this figure:

>   I rise as from a bath of sparkling water,
>   A bath of azure light, among dark rocks,
>   Out of the stream of sound.[6]

As an example of the accumulation of varied sounds, the following from *Hellas* may be cited:

>   The sound
>   As of the assault of an imperial city
>   The hiss of inextinguishable fire,
>   The roar of giant cannon; the earth-quaking

---

[1] *Prometheus Unbound*, II. ii. 24–63. [2] *Ibid.*, II. v. 72–110. [3] *Ibid.*, II. v. 4.
[4] *Ibid.*, IV. 134.   [5] *Ibid.*, II. iv. 79.   [6] *Ibid.*, IV. 503–05.

Fall of vast bastions and precipitous towers,
The shock of crags shot from strange enginery,
The clash of wheels, and clang of armèd hoofs
And crash of brazen mail, as of the wreck
Of adamantine mountains; the mad blast
Of trumpets, and the neigh of raging steeds,
And shrieks of women whose thrill jars the blood,
And one sweet laugh, most horrible to hear,
As of a joyous infant waked, and playing
With its dead mother's breast; and now more loud
The mingled battle-cry — ha! hear I not
"'Ἐν τούτω νίκη!" "Allah-illa-Allah!"? [7]

I shall now take up an act of the *Prometheus Unbound* and list the allusions to sounds which it contains. Almost any act would be conclusive as to Shelley's proclivity, but I have chosen the second as particularly rich in passages:

1. The Aeolian music of the sea-green plumes of Panthea winnows the crimson dawn near the end of Asia's first speech.[8]

2. Music is spoken of in line 51.

3. A voice falls like music in lines 65 and 66.

4. "Footsteps of weak melody" and "many sounds" are heard.[9]

5. Asia tells of the dream in which the wind shook "clinging music from the boughs" and sounds bade her follow.[10]

6. Echoes are now introduced, speak like persons, and fill a long passage with their melody.[11]

[7] *Hellas*, 814–29. [8] *Prometheus Unbound*, II. i. 25–27.
[9] *Ibid.*, II. i. 88–92. [10] *Ibid.*, II. i. 156–62. [11] *Ibid.*, II. i. 162–208.

7. In the second scene, the long passage of thirty-nine lines above quoted, in which the song of the nightingale and the eddies of the echoes are dilated upon, fills up the second and third choruses; the allusion continues for two more lines.

8. A little further on the "wise and lovely songs" of "thwart Silenus" are extolled.[12]

9. Scene iii now begins, characteristically, with the words, "Hither the sound has borne us." [13]

10. At the end of Panthea's speech two lines describe the "Evoe" of the Maenads.[14]

11. About twenty lines further down cataracts howl and avalanches resound.[15]

12. The whirling sound is mentioned in the song of the spirits.[16]

13. In the fourth scene winds and loved voices are mentioned.[17]

14. The howling of Pain.[18]

15. The invention of speech and music.[19]

16. "A voice is wanting." [20]

17. In the fifth scene the Earth whispers.[21]

18. Sounds in the air and Panthea's words are described.[22]

19. Asia's voice is the theme of the third stanza of a song.[23]

20. Last of all comes the long passage [24] previously

[12] *Ibid.*, II. ii. 91–97.
[13] *Ibid.*, II. iii. 1.
[14] *Ibid.*, II. iii. 9–10.
[15] *Ibid.*, II. iii. 33–42.
[16] *Ibid.*, II. iii. 63.
[17] *Ibid.*, II. iv. 12–14.
[18] *Ibid.*, II. iv. 26–27.
[19] *Ibid.*, II. iv. 72–79.
[20] *Ibid.*, II. iv. 115–16.
[21] *Ibid.*, II. v. 3.
[22] *Ibid.*, II. v. 35–41.
[23] *Ibid.*, II. v. 60–65.
[24] *Ibid.*, II. v. 72–110.

mentioned, occupying the rest of the act and describing how Asia's soul is an enchanted boat floating upon the silver waves of sweet singing.

The act contains 687 lines: of these 188 or more than one-fourth are devoted to the exposition of sound.

Shelley is very fond of minute or tenuous sounds.

> Low, sweet, faint sounds, like the farewell of ghosts [25]

> The small clear silver lute of the young Spirit
> That sits i' the morning star [26]

> By the small, still, sweet spirit of that sound [27]

> Listen too,
> How every pause is filled with under-notes,
> Clear, silver, icy, keen awakening tones,[28]

Shelley is no exception to the rule that lovers of sound are also lovers of silence. When he wishes to impress us with the terror of the howl of cataracts, he tells us that it is "awful as silence." [29] In the same vein he speaks of "solemn midnight's tingling silentness." [30] The vocality of silence could not escape so impressionable a spirit:

> When night makes a weird sound of its own stillness [31]

After the powerful yet poetical realism of the above line, the descent to so mere an intellectual trinket as the following is sufficiently marked:

> And Silence, too enamoured of that voice,
> Locks its mute music in her rugged cell.[32]

[25] *Ibid.*, II. i. 158.
[26] *Ibid.*, III. ii. 38–39.
[27] *Epipsychidion*, 331.
[28] *Prometheus Unbound*, IV. 188–90.
[29] *Ibid.*, II. iii. 36.
[30] *Alastor*, 7.
[31] *Ibid.*, 30.
[32] *Ibid.*, 65–66.

For this levity, however, Milton's "Silence was took ere she was ware"[33] must be held partly responsible,

Queen Mab ought to be forgiven for all its heterodoxies for the sake of the delightful line, "The lovely silence of the unfathomed main."[34]

The following is noteworthy:

> sounds of air,
> Folded in cells of crystal silence there.[35]

Powerful and noble sound is adequately handled.

> What is that awful sound?
> *Panthea.* 'Tis the deep music of the rolling world,
> Kindling within the strings of the waved air
> Aeolian modulations.[36]

> Thou breathe into the many-folded shell,
> Loosening its mighty music; it shall be
> As thunder mingled with clear echoes;[37]

Sounds of terror are strongly pictured:

> In a cavern under is fettered the thunder,
> It struggles and howls at fits.[38]

> The sound is of whirlwind underground,
> Earthquake, and fire, and mountains cloven;
> The shape is awful, like the sound,[39]

Compare the unequaled power and dignity of the following:

> So as I stood, one blast of muttering thunder
> Burst in far peals along the waveless deep[40]

---

[33] *Comus*, 557–58.   [34] iv. 95.   [35] *The Witch of Atlas*, xiv. 2–3.
[36] *Prometheus Unbound*, IV. 185–88.   [37] *Ibid.*, III. iii. 80–82.
[38] *The Cloud*, 19–20.   [39] *Prometheus Unbound*, I. 231–33.
[40] *The Revolt of Islam*, I. ii. 1–2.

In *A Vision of the Sea* he speaks of an "earthquake of sound."[41] In his conception of sound there was a purity, a clarity, the happy effects of which were not least felt when the sound was mighty and terrific. In estimating Shelley's sense of the power of sound the description of the effects of the curse of Prometheus in the opening of the drama must be taken into account. His sensibility to the milder appeals to the sense of hearing is described in terms which would brand a man less sincere and less sensitive with the charge of rhetorical exaggeration.

> My brain is wild, my breath comes quick —
>   The blood is listening in my frame,
> And thronging shadows, fast and thick,
>   Fall on my overflowing eyes;
> My heart is quivering like a flame;
>   As morning dew, that in the sunbeam dies,
>   I am dissolved in these consuming ecstasies.[42]

As echoes are a rarefaction or attenuation of sound, as they represent a withdrawal of sound in the direction of the mysterious and the impalpable, their hold on Shelley should logically have been strong, and the evidence is corroborative of this notion. We have seen that they are introduced as actors and speakers in the conclusion of the first scene of the second act of *Prometheus Unbound*. Echo, personified in the Greek form, is elaborately described in stanza xv of *Adonais*. The incidental allusions are numerous and strongly marked.

---
[41] Line 9.
[42] *To Constantia, Singing*, iii. 5–11.

Odor

A LOVE OF odor is perhaps more readily noted than a love of light or sound. An extraordinary pleasure in these latter manifestations may be slightly obscured by the fact that the ordinary pleasure in them is itself great, and the exaggeration of the large is less noticeable than that of the little. One is very quick, therefore, in finding out that Shelley's delight in smell is remarkable; that his poetry steals and gives odor with an eagerness worthy of

> the sweet South
> That breathes upon a bank of violets.

He cannot dwell upon fragrance so sedulously as upon light and sound, for odor is less susceptible of transference to the spoken word or the printed page than the appeals to the higher senses. It has not that variety and precision of matter which enables literature to avail itself of the reports of sight, nor that affinity of nature which likewise qualifies literature — itself sound or the record of sound — to deal adequately with the reports of hearing. Sensations of smell are relatively homogeneous, monotonous, and untranslatable into the form of language. Nobody can enlarge upon an odor. The love of smells must be indicated not by copiousness of description or minuteness of detail, but by frequency of affectionate reference. Let us see if Shelley supplies this indication.

In *Rosalind and Helen* between lines 961 and 1110, that is, within the space of 149 lines, there are five allusions to odor:

> And there were odours then to make
> The very breath we did respire
> A liquid element [1]

> When the summer wind faint odours brought
> From mountain flowers [2]

> And she brought crowns of sea-buds white
> Whose odour is so sweet and faint [3]

> And rare Arabian odours came,
> Through the myrtle copses, steaming thence
> From the hissing frankincense, [4]

> And now to the hushed ear it floats
> Like field-smells known in infancy [5]

The first section of *The Sensitive Plant* comprises 114 lines; it contains eight allusions to odor.

> And their breath was mixed with fresh odour, sent
> From the turf, like the voice and the instrument [6]

> music so delicate, soft, and intense,
> It was felt like an odour within the sense [7]

> the sweet tuberose,
> The sweetest flower for scent that blows [8]

> For each one was interpenetrated
> With the light and the odour its neighbour shed [9]

---

[1] *Rosalind and Helen*, 961–63.
[2] *Ibid.*, 1015–16.
[3] *Ibid.*, 1081–82.
[4] *Ibid.*, 1089–91.
[5] *Ibid.*, 1109–10.
[6] *The Sensitive Plant*, i. 15–16.
[7] *Ibid.*, i. 27–28.
[8] *Ibid.*, i. 37–38.
[9] *Ibid.*, i. 66–67.

> Radiance and odour are not its dower [10]
>
> The plumèd insects swift and free
> Like golden boats on a sunny sea,
> Laden with light and odour.[11]
>
> Each cloud faint with the fragrance it bears [12]
>
> > In which every sound, and odour, and beam,
> > Move, as reeds in a single stream [13]

I do not cite these two lists of passages as typical; they are the extremes: but even as extremes they are all but conclusive. Once he abandons himself to the wildest caprices of fancy in describing the odors of *The Witch of Atlas*.

> And odours in a kind of aviary
>   Of ever-blooming Eden-trees she kept,
> Clipt in a floating net, a love-sick Fairy
>   Had woven from dew-beams while the moon yet slept;
> As bats at the wired window of a dairy,
>   They beat their vans; and each was an adept,
> When loosed and missioned, making wings of winds,
> To stir sweet thoughts or sad, in destined minds.[14]

I add a few more examples from well-known poems:

>   and fill
> . . . .
> With living hues and odours plain and hill [15]
>
> > Like a rose embowered
> >   In its own green leaves,
> > By warm winds deflowered,

---

[10] *Ibid.*, i. 75. [11] *Ibid.*, i. 82–84.
[12] *Ibid.*, i. 89. [13] *Ibid.*, i. 92–93.
[14] Stanza xvi. [15] *Ode to the West Wind*, i. 10–12.

ODOR

> Till the scent it gives
> Makes faint with too much sweet these
>   heavy-wingèd thieves:[16]

> Music when soft voices die,
> Vibrates in the memory —
> Odours, when sweet violets sicken,
> Live within the sense they quicken[17]

> And the Champak's odours fail
> Like sweet thoughts in a dream[18]

> And gentle odours led my steps astray,
>   Mixed with a sound of waters murmuring[19]

The odors that chiefly appealed to Shelley were those of flowers, of spice, and of the spring air or sod. He rarely or never mentions the odor of fruit, or of food of any kind. Odor was to him an acute form of that revelation or emanation of love which became to him the supreme fact in the economy of the universe. It induced a mood of voluptuous languor, often associated with the word "faint," and acting in some cases perhaps as a sedative rather than a stimulant to his imaginative powers. It was largely as a breath or exhalation, the expression of a beautiful object in a form which made it poignant to one sense while it withdrew it from the scrutiny of all the others, the union of intensity and elusiveness so often referred to, that constituted its fascination for Shelley.

---

[16] *To a Skylark*, 51–55.
[17] *To——*, "Music when soft voices die," 1–4.
[18] *The Indian Serenade*, ii. 3–4.
[19] *The Question*, i. 3–4.

It is noteworthy, though hardly singular, that in odor, as well as in other points, the ardor of Shelley's devotion to the beautiful permitted him not only to be keenly sensitive to the ugly and the revolting but even to dwell with a sort of perverse relish on manifestations of this sort in his poetry. In *The Sensitive Plant* we find the following:

> a northern whirlwind wandering about
> Like a wolf that had smelt a dead child out [20]

> And the smell, cold, oppressive, and dank,
> Sent through the pores of the coffin plank.[21]

[20] iii. 106–07. [21] iii. 11–12.

Coordination

IT IS A very significant fact that Shelley often refers not only to luminous and sonorous and odoriferous objects, but very often also to the abstract or generalized property. He says not merely sun, star, and firefly, but light; not merely sigh, song, or crash, but sound; not merely tuberose or sandalwood, but odor. He is equaled by few poets, and I doubt if he is exceeded by any, in the frequency of his recurrence to these abstract terms. Now as light is a less palpable, more elusive notion than sun, as odor and sound are less palpable and more elusive than warble or cassia, the confirmation which the above fact offers to the theory I have propounded of Shelley's tastes is obvious and important. Another habit which has a kindred though inferior significance is the coupling or even the trebling and quadrupling of these abstract terms, motion, life, or the like being drawn upon to supply the fourth corner to the quadrilateral. When the conception "light" has reached the point of ready combination with the conception "sound" or "odor," it seems clear that both ideas have lost another portion of their original concreteness, a portion distinct from that previously lost in the transition from the ideas "sun," "cry," "frankincense," to the ideas "light," "sound," "odor." The examples which follow illustrate both the generalizing and the coordinating habit. I class light, hue, and color as a single form of generalization.

Couplets

A. Sight and sound.

> Like hues and harmonies of evening [1]
>
> light and music [2]
>
> light and sound ebbed from the earth [3]
>
> yet through all its mass
> Flow as through empty space, music and light: [4]
>
> And around them the soft stream did glide and dance
> With a motion of sweet sound and radiance [5]
>
> Whose waters like blithe light and music are [6]
>
> Whose coming is as light and music are
> 'Mid dissonance and gloom [7]

Just below this in the same sentence we have with reference to one object:

> a gentle tone
> Among rude voices, a beloved light [8]
>
> An echo and a light unto eternity [9]
>
> an ocean of splendour and harmony [10]

Compare:

> With lightning and with music [11]

---

[1] *Hymn to Intellectual Beauty*, i. 8. [2] *Ode to Naples*, 108.
[3] *Rosalind and Helen*, 970. [4] *Prometheus Unbound*, IV. 239–40.
[5] *The Sensitive Plant*, i. 47–48. [6] *Epipsychidion*, 59.
[7] *Ibid.*, canceled passage, 72–73. [8] *Ibid.*, 75–76.
[9] *Adonais*, i. 9. [10] *Prometheus Unbound*, IV. 134.
[11] *Adonais*, xii. 5.

COORDINATION

B. Sight and odor.

> Like an air-dissolved star
> Mingling light and fragrance [12]

> living hues and odours [13]

> scent and hue [14]

> But the Sensitive Plant has no bright flower;
> Radiance and odour are not its dower [15]

> The plumèd insects swift and free,
> Like golden boats on a sunny sea,
> Laden with light and odour [16]

> the light and odour of its [friendship's] bloom [17]

It is as the odour and the colour of the rose to the texture of the elements which compose it.[18]

> whose shade cast
> Darkness and odours [19]

C. Sound and odor.

> wild sounds and odours [20]

> love and odour and deep melody [21]

II. TRIPLETS

> The sound of their oceans, the light of their sky,
> The music and fragrance their solitudes breathe [22]

> Odours and gleams and murmurs [23]

---

[12] *Euganean Hills*, 289–90.
[13] *Ode to the West Wind*, i. 12.
[14] *Song of Proserpine*, ii. 3.
[15] *The Sensitive Plant*, i. 74–75.
[16] *Ibid.*, i. 82–84.
[17] *Epipsychidion*, canceled passage, 70.
[18] *A Defence of Poetry*, p. 136.
[19] *The Witch of Atlas*, XXXV. iii. 3–4.
[20] *The Revolt of Islam*, XII. xxxiii. 5.
[21] *Prometheus Unbound*, IV. 330.
[22] *Hellas*, 1055–56.
[23] *The Woodman and the Nightingale*, 61.

> the light
> Of wave-reflected flowers, and floating odours
> And music soft [24]
>
> The quivering vapours of dim noontide,
> Which like a sea o'er the warm earth glide,
> In which every sound, and odour, and beam,
> Move, as reeds in a single stream; [25]

Let the reader try to frame for himself a clear picture of the image in the last two lines. If I mistake not he will find the task difficult, and his difficulty may be in a sort the measure of the extent to which the ideas of light and sound and odor were attenuated and etherealized in the mind of Shelley.

The following are slightly different combinations:

> With ever changing sound and light and foam [26]
>
> in form,
> Sound, colour [27]
>
> Where music and moonlight and feeling
>   Are one [28]
>
> light, sound, and motion [29]
>
> A maze of light and life and motion [30]

III. Larger Combinations

> All he had loved and moulded into thought
> From shape, and hue, and odour, and sweet sound,
> Lamented Adonais [31]

---

[24] *Prometheus Unbound*, III. ii. 31–33.
[25] *The Sensitive Plant*, i. 90–93.
[26] *Epipsychidion*, 431.
[27] *Ibid.*, 210–11.
[28] *To Jane*, "The keen stars are twinkling," 5–6.
[29] *A Summer Evening Churchyard*, 9.
[30] *Rosalind and Helen*, 129.
[31] *Adonais*, xiv. 1–3.

And every motion, odour, beam, and tone,
With that deep music is in unison [32]

And soft sunshine, and the sound
Of old forests echoing round,
And the light and smell divine
Of all flowers that breathe and shine: [33]

Be it love, light, harmony,
Odour, or the soul of all [34]

[22] *Epipsychidion*, 453-54.   [33] *Euganean Hills*, 348-51.
[34] *Ibid.*, 315-16.

Assimilation

But the mere conjunction or collocation of light, sound, odor, and their correlates is not enough for Shelley; he must unite them still more closely by means of comparison, or even by a kind of fusion, identification, or transformation of one into the other. To elucidate the objects which appeal to one sense by illustrations drawn from objects that appeal to others, to compare sights to sounds, sights to odors, sounds to odors, or vice versa is a practice of some rarity in literature and is a clear indication of an appetite for the subtle and impalpable. The point of resemblance between a sight and a sound can be found only in the remotest and most highly rarefied and spiritualized property of each, since in all other respects their unlikeness is glaring Shelley's proneness to this form of simile is extraordinary, if not unexampled; I remember no other author in whom it occurs with like frequency. Dante's phrase *dove il sol tace*[1] applied to sunset is startling enough to be itself almost a demonstration of the rarity of this species of comparison. Cases like Shakespeare's

> The setting sun, and music at the close,
> As the last taste of sweets, is sweetest last[2]

though not uncommon, are hardly to the point, since in this case the resemblance is not found in the quality

[1] *Inferno*, i. 60.   [2] *Richard II*, II. i. 12-13.

of the sensation, but merely in those variations of intensity which are common to the most diverse phenomena. The comparisons that I now proceed to abduce from Shelley are mostly of a totally different nature.

A. Sight to sound.

> See the pale azure fading into silver
> Lining it with soft yet glowing light:
> Looks it not like lulled music sleeping there? [3]

Again with majestic beauty:

> the far flashing of their starry lances
> Reverberates the dying light of day [4]

> And in quick smiles whose light would come and go
> Like music o'er wide waves [5]

> to live again in looks, which dart
> With the thrilling tone into the voiceless heart [6]

Take the following rare and strange expression applied to the planet Venus:

> The sphere whose light is melody to lovers [7]

B. Sound to sight.

> its music long,
> Like woven sounds of streams and breezes, held
> His inmost sense suspended in its web
> Of many-coloured woof and shifting hues. [8]

Or in the beautiful simile from the *Skylark,*

> All the earth and air
> With thy voice is loud,

---

[3] *Prometheus Unbound,* III. iii. 71–73.
[4] *Hellas,* 331–32.
[5] *The Revolt of Islam,* XII. xxxvii. 4–5.
[6] *Epipsychidion,* 562–63.
[7] *The Triumph of Life,* 479.
[8] *Alastor,* 154–57.

138 POWER AND ELUSIVENESS IN SHELLEY

> As, when night is bare,
> From one lonely cloud
> The moon rains out her beams, and Heaven is overflowed.[9]

In the stanza preceding this, the bird's song is compared to another phase of moonlight and, in the succeeding stanza, to bright drops flowing from rainbow clouds.[10] In *Adonais* fading melodies are compared to flowers:

> while one, with soft enamoured breath,
> Rekindled all the fading melodies,
> With which, like flowers that mock the corse beneath,
> He had adorned and hid the coming bulk of death.[11]

The above simile is rather curious in the fact that not merely the flowers and the corpse are figurative but the relation of the melodies to the idea of death is itself partly metaphorical, in the implied likeness between material and intellectual things so characteristic of Shelley, in the complication of the picture by the introduction of the idea of fire in "rekindled," and its further complication by the portrayal of death, who ought logically to be lying down, as a "coming bulk."

The same comparison of music to flowers is given in a daintily compact form in *Epipsychidion*:

> This song shall be thy rose [12]

> And music from her respiration spread
> Like light.[13]

Music is compared to light again in *The Revolt of Islam:*

---

[9] *To a Skylark*, 26–30.   [10] *Ibid.*, 21–25, 33–35.
[11] ii. 6–9.   [12] Line 9.   [13] Lines 329–30.

ASSIMILATION

> To feel the dreamlike music, which did swim
> >Like beams through floating clouds on waves below,
> Falling in pauses from that Altar dim,[14]

The following passage is much to the purpose, if "liquid splendour" be taken, as seems to me most probable, to refer to the voice:

> Fair are others; none beholds thee,
> >But thy voice sounds low and tender
> Like the fairest, for it folds thee
> >From the sight, that liquid splendour,[15]
>
> >>As o'er the mountains of the earth
> From peak to peak leap on the beams of Morning's birth:
> So from that cry over the boundless hills,
> >Sudden was caught one universal sound,[16]
>
> Clear, silver, icy, keen awakening tones,
> Which pierce the sense, and live within the soul,
> As the sharp stars pierce winter's crystal air
> And gaze upon themselves within the sea.[17]

He liked this so well that a like thought is embodied in less powerful verse further on in the same act of the *Prometheus:*

> Oh, gentle Moon, the voice of thy delight
> Falls on me like thy clear and tender light
> Soothing the seaman, borne the summer night
> >Through isles for ever calm;[18]
>
> See where the spirits of the human mind
> Wrapped in sweet sounds as in bright veils approach[19]

---
[14] *The Revolt of Islam*, V. xli. 6–8.   [15] *Prometheus Unbound*, II. v. 60–63.
[16] *The Revolt of Islam*, IX. iii. 8–9; iv. 1–2.
[17] *Prometheus Unbound*, IV. 190–93.   [18] *Ibid.*, IV. 495–98.   [19] *Ibid.*, IV. 81–82.

C. Sound to odor. The subject is the nightingale's song:

>   suddenly
> 'Tis scattered in a thousand notes,
> And now to the hushed ear it floats
> Like field smells known in infancy,[20]

D. Odor to sound. The sincerity of the poet in these similes is shown by the precision with which the detail is sometimes carried out. In the following the union of two scents is compared to the union of two sounds:

> The snow-drop, and then the violet,
> Arose from the ground with warm rain wet,
> And their breath was mixed with fresh odour sent
> From the turf, like the voice and the instrument.[21]

E. Combinations. In the following the three senses of sight, sound, and touch are very curiously blended:

> I rise as from a bath of sparkling water,
> A bath of azure light, among dark rocks,
> Out of the stream of sound.[22]

In the following the light of a star is compared first to odor, afterwards to music, and lastly to a phenomenon of touch:

> In that star's smile, whose smile is like the scent
> Of a jonquil when evening breezes fan it,
> Or the soft note in which his dear lament
> The Brescian shepherd breathes, or the caress
> That turned his weary slumber to content; [23]

[20] *Rosalind and Helen*, 1107–10.
[21] *The Sensitive Plant*, i. 13–16.
[22] *Prometheus Unbound*, IV. 503–05.
[23] *The Triumph of Life*, 419–23.

ASSIMILATION

In the following the song of the nightingale is compared to a flood, to moonlight, and to the scents of the tuberose, the last-named being incidentally likened to clouds:

> And as a vale is watered by a flood,
> Or as the moonlight fills the open sky
> Struggling with darkness — as a tuberose
> Peoples some Indian dell with scents which lie
> Like clouds above the flower from which they rose,
> The singing of that happy nightingale [24]

I prefer to leave the reader to determine what is likened to what in the following:

> In thy dark eyes a power like light doth lie,
>   Even tho' the sounds which were thy voice, which burn
> Between thy lips, are laid to sleep;
>   Within thy breath, and on thy hair, like odour it is yet,
> And from thy touch like fire doth leap. [25]

But there are passages in which the relation becomes something more intimate than we can fitly class under the names of simile and metaphor. It is sometimes a causal relation. In the following passage a delicate fancy substitutes the melody of the wind for the wind itself as the shaping agent for the cloud.

> Its shape was such as summer melody
> Of the south wind in spicy vales might give
> To some light cloud [26]

In the same poem [27] a plant is nursed by music. Soft

---
[24] *The Woodman and the Nightingale*, 6–11.
[25] *To Constantia, Singing*, i. 3–7.
[26] *Fragments of an Unfinished Drama*, 215–17.
[27] *Ibid.*, 179–93.

melodies are played upon the flute, and tales of forgotten love and of deserted maids are sung, to quicken its powers of growth. In the *Prometheus Unbound* Ione, intoxicated by the loveliness of two spirits, exclaims, "Their beauty gives me voice" [28] — though this may be taken in a sense which robs it of any direct bearing on our point.

Again the data of one sense are transformed into those of another. The leaves of the magic plant:

> like a poet's heart
> Changing bright fancy to sweet sentiment
> Changed half the light to fragrance.[29]

It may be thought that there is as much science as fancy in this, but the following is less reconcilable with fact. Shelley is speaking of the flowers that grow out of a dead body:

> Like incarnations of the stars, when splendour
> Is changed to fragrance, they illumine death [30]

A fancy like that embodied in the subjoined stanza would have occurred to hardly any other imagination than Shelley's:

> And the hyacinth purple, and white, and blue,
> Which flung from its bells a sweet peal anew
> Of music so delicate, soft and intense,
> It was felt like an odour within the sense; [31]

Sometimes the idea is that of intermixture or fusion.

[28] I. 759.
[29] *Fragments of an Unfinished Drama*, 175–77.
[30] *Adonais*, xx. 3–4.
[31] *The Sensitive Plant*, i. 25–28.

ASSIMILATION

> Sweet streams of sunny thought, and flowers fresh-blown
> Are there, and weave their sounds and odours into one.[32]

It should be remarked that in the above both the sounds and odors are metaphorical.

The following is highly significant:

> And the wild odour of the forest flowers,
> The music of the living grass and air,
> The emerald light of leaf-entangled beams
> Round its intense yet self-conflicting speed,
> Seem kneaded into one aërial mass
> Which drowns the sense.[33]

The lines referred to above (pages 128, 134) in which the sounds and odors and beams are said to move like reeds in a single stream should be classed with these interfusions. The "maze of light and life and motion" (page 134) and the world in which "music and moonlight and feeling are one" (page 134) might be associated with these examples. The following, though less strictly to the point, are worth citing:

> Of unentangled intermixture made
> By Love, of light and motion [34]

>   thou young Dawn
> Turn all thy dew to splendour [35]

The subject merges insensibly into Shelley's pantheistic conception of the universe, which will receive notice later.

---

[32] *The Revolt of Islam*, IX. xxvi. 8-9.
[33] *Prometheus Unbound*, IV. 256-61.
[34] *Epipsychidion*, 93-94.
[35] *Adonais*, xli. 2-3.

To sum up what has been affirmed and, it is hoped, demonstrated, with respect to Shelley's use of light, sound, and odor:

1. Light, sound, and odor are among the more abstract and elusive constituents of the physical universe. Every one of them is the object of Shelley's peculiar affection and constant reference.

2. Not only are objects emitting light, sound, and odor of constant occurrence in Shelley's poetry but the abstract ideas and names themselves are found in abundance.

3. These ideas are constantly linked in pairs or terms, indicating that they are dimly and abstractly conceived.

4. The resemblances among these ideas, which reside in the most elusive form of the conception, are instanced by Shelley with great frequency.

5. The ideas are sometimes so far fused and amalgamated as to be almost deprived of individual distinction.

Penetration and Absorption

AMONG THE ideas which are at the same time powerful and mysterious, which provoke and allure but never quite satisfy the imagination, few are more interesting or more incontestable than the ideas of penetration, permeation, absorption, and dissolution. One substance or vibration passes into another by methods so unsearchable, by channels and passages so minute, that the mind is at once acutely conscious of the fact, intensely eager to realize it in a clear picture, and deeply sensible of the futility of every attempt at realization. The idea of saturation lends a perennial interest to a sponge, to the moist spring soil, to the process of vegetable growth; the word "soak," homely as it is, is fairly drenched in suggestiveness. The word "percolation" is an unfailing delight. The permeation of the air with light, of the air with moisture, of the air with fragrance, of the cloud with wind, of the cloud with light, of the water with air, of the water with light, of the earth with water, of wood with heat, of flesh with heat, of a liquid with a suspended or dissolved solid, are ideas which at once impress, baffle, and fascinate us. If we are right in our diagnosis of Shelley's mind, the interest he took in phenomena of this kind should have been exceptional. The truth of this inference can be readily shown.

In my discussion of this topic I am somewhat embarrassed by the extent to which it is intersected and overlapped by the succeeding topic of effluence. The two ideas are distinct enough, but the illustrations of effluence are often likewise illustrations of penetration, since one object naturally absorbs what another radiates. One is obliged to choose, therefore, between the iteration of examples and the truncation of one's proofs.

The subject may be fitly introduced by a long citation from *Lines written among the Euganean Hills:*

> And the plains that silent lie
> Underneath, the leaves unsodden
> Where the infant frost has trodden
> With his morning-wingèd feet,
> Whose bright print is gleaming yet;
> And the red and golden vines,
> Piercing with their trellised lines
> The rough, dark-skirted wilderness;
> The dun and bladed grass no less,
> Pointing from his hoary tower
> In the windless air; the flower
> Glimmering at my feet; the line
> Of the olive-sandalled Apennine
> In the south dimly islanded;
> And the Alps, whose snows are spread
> High between the clouds and sun;
> And of living things each one;
> And my spirit which so long
> Darkened this swift stream of song,
> Interpenetrated lie
> By the glory of the sky.[1]

[1] Lines 294-314.

PENETRATION AND ABSORPTION

In the *Prometheus Unbound* the Moon addresses the Earth in a passage which shows the strength of Shelley's imaginative grasp of these elusive and tantalizing conceptions:

> Some Spirit is darted like a beam from thee,
>   Which penetrates my frozen frame,
>   And passes with the warmth of flame,
> With love, and odour, and deep melody
>   Through me, through me! [2]

The Earth replies in a passage of equal significance:

> It interpenetrates my granite mass,
>   Through tangled roots and trodden clay doth pass,
> Into the utmost leaves and delicatest flowers;
>   Upon the winds, among the clouds 'tis spread,
>   It wakes a life in the forgotten dead,
> They breathe a spirit up from their obscurest bowers.[3]

The penetration of cloud or vapor by light never failed to touch the fancy of Shelley:

> And, as a dying meteor stains a wreath
>   Of moonlight vapour, which the cold night clips,
>   It flushed through his pale limbs, and passed
>   to its eclipse.[4]

> His cold pale limbs and pulseless arteries
> Are like the fibres of a cloud instinct
> With light,[5]

>   A mortal shape to him
>   Was like the vapour dim
> Which the orient planet animates with light [6]

---

[2] *Prometheus Unbound*, IV. 327-31. [3] *Ibid.*, IV. 370-75.
[4] *Adonais*, xii. 7-9. [5] *Hellas*, 143-45.
[6] *Ibid.*, 215-17.

> Even as a vapour fed with golden beams
> That ministered on sunlight [7]
>
> > the brightness
> Of her divinest presence trembles through
> Her limbs, as underneath a cloud of dew
> Embodied in the windless Heaven of June
> Amid the splendour-wingèd stars, the Moon
> Burns, inextinguishably beautiful: [8]
>
> > > an atmosphere
> Which wrapped me in its all-dissolving power,
> As the warm aether of the morning sun
> Wraps ere it drinks some cloud of wandering dew.
> I saw not, heard not, moved not, only felt
> His presence flow and mingle through my blood
> Till it became his life, and his grew mine,
> And I was thus absorbed,[9]
>
> Child of Light! thy limbs are burning
> > Through the vest which seems to hide them;
> As the radiant lines of morning
> > Through the clouds ere they divide them;
> And this atmosphere divinest
> Shrouds thee wheresoe'er thou shinest.[10]
>
> Let the Hours, and the spirits of might and pleasure,
> > Like the clouds and sunbeams, unite.[11]

It will be observed that in the eight passages above cited the cloud or vapor is metaphorical and represents often a body permeated by the soul here presented under the figure of light. Shelley was, in fact, almost equally sensitive to physical and moral interpenetration.

---

[7] *Alastor*, 663–64.   [8] *Epipsychidion*, 77–82.
[9] *Prometheus Unbound*, II. i. 75–82.   [10] *Ibid.*, II. v. 54–59.   [11] *Ibid.*, IV. 79–80.

PENETRATION AND ABSORPTION

The following is an interesting bit of the cloud's soliloquy:

> I pass through the pores of the ocean and shores;
> I change, but I cannot die.[12]

The Cloud suggests another idea of which Shelley is superlatively fond; the idea of dissolving or solution. His use of the words "dissolve," "dissolved," "dissolving" approaches the dimensions of a mannerism, using that word as before in a sense which excludes the idea of affectation. There are two instances in *The Cloud* itself:

> And then again I dissolve it in rain,
> And laugh as I pass in thunder [13]

> And I all the while bask in heaven's blue smile,
> Whilst he is dissolving in rains [14]

In the last ten stanzas of the *Ode to Liberty,* a space of one hundred and fifty lines, the verb occurs three times.

> Reflected, it dissolved the visions of the trance
> In which, as in a tomb, the nations lay [15]

> Her chains are threads of gold, she need but smile
> And they dissolve [16]

> As summer clouds dissolve, unburthened of their rain [17]

In *Rosalind and Helen* the verb or participle is used three times within the space of one hundred thirty lines.

[12] *The Cloud,* 75-76.   [13] *Ibid.,* 11-12.   [14] *Ibid.,* 29-30.
[15] *Ode to Liberty,* x. 8-9.   [16] *Ibid.,* xiii. 9-10.   [17] *Ibid.,* xix. 8.

> My languid fingers drew and flung
> Circles of life-dissolving sound [18]
>
> Scatters its sense-dissolving fragrance o'er
> The liquid marble of the windless lake [19]
>
> Beyond the region of dissolving rains [20]

I cite some other interesting passages:

> Heaven smiles, and faiths and empires gleam,
> Like wrecks of a dissolving dream [21]
>
> Or an air-dissolved star
> Mingling light and fragrance [22]
>
> I see the waves upon the shore,
> Like light dissolved in star-showers, thrown [23]
>
> And odours warm and fresh fell from her hair
> Dissolving the dull cold in the frore air [24]
>
> I am dissolved in these consuming ecstasies [25]
>
> since dissolved
> Into the sense with which love talks, my rest
> Was troubled and yet sweet [26]

These are Panthea's words. I have already quoted (page 73) the passage in which she describes the dream in which her spirit was dissolved by that of Prometheus, and afterwards, by a curiously matter-of-fact completion of the physical metaphor, "condensed." [27] The passage [28] in which the Moon describes the thawing of the

---

[18] *Rosalind and Helen*, 1165–66. [19] *Ibid.*, 1251–52. [20] *Ibid.*, 1296.
[21] *Hellas*, 1064–65. [22] *Euganean Hills*, 289–90.
[23] *Stanzas written in Dejection near Naples*, ii. 3–4.
[24] *Epipsychidion*, 333–34. [25] *To Constantia, Singing*, iii. 11.
[26] *Prometheus Unbound*, II. i. 52–54. [27] *Ibid.*, II. i. 86. [28] *Ibid.*, IV. 424–36.

PENETRATION AND ABSORPTION

shroud of frost and sleep that invested her orb and the Earth replies by likening the change to that undergone by a "half-unfrozen dew-globe" in the "dissolving warmth of dawn" is also interesting.

Drinking, chiefly in metaphor, is not uncommon.

Drinking from thy sense and sight
Beauty, majesty, and might,[29]

Through whose o'ershadowing woods I wandered once
With Asia, drinking life from her loved eyes [30]

Or the warm aether of the morning sun
Wraps ere it drinks some cloud of wandering dew [31]

The interpenetration of the light and odor of different flowers with one another is thus noted:

For each one was interpenetrated
With the light and the odour its neighbor shed,
Like young lovers whom youth and love make dear
Wrapped and filled by their mutual atmosphere.[32]

A curious sort of bacteriology is exemplified in the threat uttered by the Furies to Prometheus:

Thou think'st we will live through thee, one by one
Like animal life . . . .
. . . .
That we will be dread thought beneath thy brain,
And foul desire round thine astonisht heart,
And blood within thy labyrinthine veins
Crawling like agony [33]

One sound is penetrated by another:

[29] *Ibid.*, IV. 481–82.   [30] *Ibid.*, I. 122–23.
[31] *Ibid.*, II. i. 77–78.   [32] *The Sensitive Plant*, i. 66–69.
[33] *Prometheus Unbound*, I. 483–91.

> all other sounds were penetrated
> By the small, still sweet spirit of that sound [34]

A shell is penetrated with light:

> The boat was one curved shell of hollow pearl,
> Almost translucent with the light divine
> Of her within.[35]

The following are cases of moral penetration:

> I stood, and felt the dawn of my long night
> Was penetrating me with living light [36]

> Soon the solemn mood
> Of her pure mind kindled through all her frame
> A permeating fire: [37]

The union of bodies and of spirits, both of which were profoundly interesting to Shelley, may be comprised under this head. Those who wish to verify the fact of Shelley's keen interest in the bodily conjunction of the sexes are referred to *The Revolt of Islam,* Canto VI, stanzas xxvii to xlv; *Rosalind and Helen,* lines 949 to 987; the central idea and various speeches in *The Cenci;* the passage in *Prometheus Unbound,* Act III, scene iv, lines 86 to 96; *The Witch of Atlas,* stanzas xxxv to xlv and lxxvi to lxxvii; the plot and many allusions in *Swellfoot;* the *Epithalamium;* and the close of *Epipsychidion.* There is little value in speculation on topics in which certainty, or even any approach to it, is out of reach, but my own reading has led me to think that Shelley's interest in these matters was the interest

---

[34] *Epipsychidion,* 330–31.
[35] *The Revolt of Islam,* XII. xxi. 1–3.
[36] *Epipsychidion,* 341–42.
[37] *Alastor,* 161–63.

PENETRATION AND ABSORPTION 153

of a poet, not of an animal, that the bodily tie between man and woman appealed to him on its typical and emblematic side far more than on the side of sensual rapture. The reality of the interest in the physical fact is, however, unquestionable, and its existence is another proof of the charm which ideas of intermixture and penetration exercised upon the mind of Shelley.

The idea of spiritual union, of identification or coalescence of one spirit with another, was profoundly attractive and is expressed in language of singular emphasis and daring. Interpenetration becomes complete in proportion as the substances which experience it are fluid, porous, and ethereal, and as souls are commonly conceived as the possessors in the highest degree of these qualifications, they are regarded as the most proper subjects for commixture or interfusion. Examples follow:

> Thou hast discovered some enchantment old,
> Whose spells have stolen my spirit as I slept
> And mingled it with thine: [38]

The infusion of the life of Prometheus into Panthea, the culmination of which is expressed in the emphatic words, "And I was thus absorbed,"[39] has been already referred to (page 148). The presence of Asia is of force to transform and to beatify the world, yet it is so dependent upon assimilation with the soul of Prometheus that it would fade if it ceased to be mingled with his.

> the aether
> Of her transforming presence, which would fade
> If it were mingled not with thine [40]

---

[88] *Prometheus Unbound*, II. i. 100–02. [39] *Ibid.*, II. i. 82. [40] *Ibid.*, I. 831–33.

Jupiter is similarly blent with Thetis:

> veiled in the light
> Of the desire which makes thee one with me,
> Thetis, bright image of eternity! [41]

I have already quoted (page 151) the passage in which the interpenetration of the light and odor of flowers is compared to young lovers "wrapped and filled by their mutual atmosphere." [42] The same ideas are expressed with even more passionate emphasis in the *Epipsychidion:*

> These names, though dear, could paint not, as is due,
> How beyond refuge I am thine. Ah me!
> I am not thine: I am a part of *thee*.[43]

At the end of the poem, having described the union of breaths and bosoms and heart-beats, he proceeds to declare that the fountains of their deepest life

> shall be
> Confused in Passion's golden purity [44]

But this is not enough; the tide of passion and insistence carries him further yet:

> We shall become the same, we shall be one
> Spirit within two frames, oh! wherefore two? [45]

The passions in their hearts are to grow till the hearts themselves, like blending meteors, "touch, mingle, are transfigured." [46] Like the meteors they find food in each other's substance, and again the paean of unity rises; the

[41] *Ibid.*, III. i. 34–36.
[42] *The Sensitive Plant*, i. 66–69.
[43] *Epipsychidion*, 50–52.
[44] *Ibid.*, 570–71.
[45] *Ibid.*, 573–74.
[46] *Ibid.*, 578.

PENETRATION AND ABSORPTION 155

expression "one hope within two wills" is made use of, only to be instantly cast aside as inadequate and replaced by "one will beneath two overshadowing minds."[47] After this it seems very little to be assured that there is to be one life, one death,

> One Heaven, one Hell, one immortality,
> And one annihilation.[48]

In the vehemence, almost turbulence, of these crowded reiterations there is something far more akin to the restlessness of a mind striving to convince itself than to the repose of achieved and assured conviction. We may agree with Dr. Brandes, so far at least as to think it highly probable that Shelley sought always, and sought always in vain, throughout his life for the achievement of this perfect and lasting union. Difference of sex must be regarded, I think, merely as the starting-place, the point of vantage, the useful but nonessential foothold, from which his mind set forth on its ill-starred but lofty and tireless quest. The hopelessness of his dream is evinced in the fact that he could even for a moment regard persons like Elizabeth Hitchener and Emilia Viviani as the destined instruments of its realization. The point which is vital to the present discussion is the lifelong pursuit of an ideal which expressed itself in terms of interpenetration, mutual absorption, and assimilation. Only a mind to whom these ideas were superlatively attractive would have given harbor and nurture to such an ideal.

[47] *Ibid.*, 570–71. [48] *Ibid.*, 585–86.

Effluence

AN EFFLUENCE, for my purpose, may be regarded as anything of a relatively light and impalpable nature proceeding from another object or substance of a nature relatively solid and tangible. Light, sound, and odor are forms of effluence, but their importance has called for specific and distinct treatment, and I group under this head some of the less definite or less understood forms of the general phenomenon. The relation to penetration and absorption has been already indicated.

That an object should emit or produce something finer than itself, and afterwards perhaps be related by contact or influence to its own emissions, are processes that could not fail to impress a mind devoted to the pursuit of the elusive and the powerful. If we are right in our view of Shelley, his interest in effluence should be profound. The first phase which I shall take up is that of shadow.

I. Shadow. We have here an appearance which at the same time attracts and eludes the imagination, which is both common and permanent, yet never ceases to be associated in our minds with figment and unreality, which has become indeed the symbol of the impalpable and the unsubstantial. Let us observe the extent to which it figures in the poems of Shelley.

In *Rosalind and Helen* shadow or its compounds is used three times within thirty-five lines:

EFFLUENCE

> Past woe its shadow backward threw [1]

> For his cheek became, not pale, but fair,
> As rose-o'ershadowed lilies are [2]

> The shadow of that slumber deep [3]

In the same poem in another place it is used three times within forty-six lines:

> where the shore
> Is shadowed with steep rocks [4]

> [cleave] with their shadows the clear depths below [5]

> And in their union soon their parents saw
> The shadow of the peace denied to them [6]

In the second act of *Prometheus Unbound* it is used five times within one hundred and twenty-one lines:

> The shadow of that soul by which I live, [7]

> more fair than aught but her
> Whose shadow thou art [8]

> the overpowering light
> Of that immortal shape was shadowed o'er
> By love [9]

Observe, for the fact is characteristic, that Panthea just above wears the shadow of the soul of Prometheus, and is here herself represented as the shadow of Asia.

> what canst thou see
> But thine own fairest shadow imaged there? [10]

> the shadow of the morning clouds, [11]

---

[1] *Rosalind and Helen*, 805.   [2] *Ibid.*, 819–20.   [3] *Ibid.*, 839.
[4] *Ibid.*, 1245–46.   [5] *Ibid.*, 1248.   [6] *Ibid.*, 1290–91.
[7] *Prometheus Unbound*, II. i. 31.   [8] *Ibid.*, II. i. 69–70.   [9] *Ibid.*, II. i. 71–73.
[10] *Ibid.*, II. i. 112–13.   [11] *Ibid.*, II. i. 151.

We may properly add to this Asia's: "I see a shade, a shape,"[12] thus making a total of six references in the space of one hundred and twenty-one lines.

Between lines 424 and 453 of the fourth act of *Prometheus Unbound,* a passage embracing four antistrophic stanzas, there are three allusions to shadows.[13] It is interesting to note that as repetitions of sound in the form of echoes become characters and speakers in the second act of the drama, so repetitions of shapes under the name of shadows become characters and speakers in the fourth act. The stage direction is: "A Train of Dark Forms and Shadows passes by confusedly, singing."[14]

The word is used three times in two stanzas, eighteen lines, of *The Revolt of Islam*.[15] In the *Hymn to Intellectual Beauty,* containing eighty-four lines, shadows are thrice mentioned; first in the noble opening,

> The awful shadow of some unseen Power
> Floats though unseen amongst us[16]

The two other cases are in the fourth and fifth stanzas.[17] *The Triumph of Life* contains 544 lines: I have marked eighteen references to shades or shadows, a ratio of one reference to a very little more than every thirty lines. In brief, the word follows Shelley like a shadow. I doubt if his record in this respect can be approached, much less paralleled, by any other poet.

II. Smiles. A smile may properly be described as an effluence, at least so far as the purposes of poetry are

---

[12] *Ibid.*, II. i. 120.   [13] *Ibid.*, IV. 424, 448, 453.
[14] *Ibid.*, IV. 8.   [15] III. xvi–xvii.
[16] i. 1–2.   [17] iv. 10; v. 11.

involved. Its impalpableness, its evanescence, its beauty, and its conveyance of joyous and, more particularly, of tender, sentiment were all strong claims on the interest of Shelley. His pages fairly dimple with smiles. *Adonais* is an elegy, and a decidedly melancholy elegy. Smiles are, therefore, the last thing which we should expect to figure conspicuously among its incidental allusions. Let us see how the facts bear out this expectation. The close of stanza xlix contains the delightful lines:

> Where like an infant's smile, over the dead,
> A light of laughing flowers along the grass is spread [18]

Stanza l contains the less resplendent but hardly less beautiful lines:

> A field is spread, on which a newer band,
> Have pitched in Heaven's smile their camp of death [19]

In stanza liii we have:

> The soft sky smiles, — the low wind whispers near [20]

Stanza liv begins

> That Light whose smile kindles the Universe [21]

Within the space of thirty-eight lines in an elegiac poem we have four uses of the word "smile," a record-breaking computation.

The showing in *Rosalind and Helen* is so significant that I am tempted at some expense of space and time to give the list of allusions entire.

> beckoned with a meaning smile [22]

---

[18] *Adonais*, xlix. 8–9.   [19] *Ibid.*, l. 7–8.   [20] *Ibid.*, liii. 7.
[21] *Ibid.*, liv. 1.   [22] *Rosalind and Helen*, 92.

> Helen smiled [23]
>
> But I could smile, and I could sleep [24]
>
> He smiled with such a woeful smile [25]
>
> love and smiles [26]

and only seven lines below:

> And watch the growing soul beneath
> Dawn in faint smiles [27]

then the characteristic phrase

> Youth's starlight smile [28]
>
> the priests, whose hatred fell
> Like the unseen blight of a smiling day [29]
>
> Ah, smiles and joyance quickly died [30]

Again only five lines below appears the following simile for blighted public hopes:

> As a summer flower that blows too soon
> Droops in the smile of the waning moon [31]

We have only nineteen lines to traverse before reaching

> And smiled again at festivals.[32]

Thirty lines more and we have:

> Serenest smiles were wont to keep [33]
>
> And smiles, — as when the lightning's blast [34]

Later on, a tear

> Would gather in the light serene

---

[23] *Ibid.*, 186. [24] *Ibid.*, 227. [25] *Ibid.*, 317. [26] *Ibid.*, 375.
[27] *Ibid.*, 382–83. [28] *Ibid.*, 480. [29] *Ibid.*, 675–76. [30] *Ibid.*, 691.
[31] *Ibid.*, 695–96. [32] *Ibid.*, 715. [33] *Ibid.*, 745. [34] *Ibid.*, 787.

> Of smiles, whose lustre bright and soft
> Beneath lay undulating there.[35]

> his mute and faded smile [36]

> And the softest strain of music made
> Sweet smiles, yet sad, arise and fade [37]

> > smiles which faintly could express
> > A mingled pain and tenderness [38]

We have here seventeen references in a poem of 1318 lines, an average of one to about seventy-seven lines.

The smiles of children had a supreme interest for Shelley. "Youth's starlight smile" quoted above is balanced by "The starlight smile of children" [39] in *The Revolt of Islam*. The dedication to the same poem contains the charming allusion to his own children:

> And from thy side two gentle babes are born
> To fill our home with smiles [40]

Earlier, no doubt in allusion as before to his own child:[41]

> Thou in the grave shall rest — yet till the phantoms flee
> > Which that house and heath and garden made dear to thee erewhile,
> Thy remembrance, and repentance, and deep musings are not free
> From the music of two voices and the light of one sweet smile.[42]

---

[35] *Ibid.*, 831–33. [36] *Ibid.*, 912. [37] *Ibid.*, 1021–22.
[38] *Ibid.*, 1058–59. [39] *The Revolt of Islam*, II. i. 1. [40] *Ibid.*, ix. 5–6.
[41] I find that Professor Dowden does not take this view, referring the two voices and the smile to Harriet Boinville and Cornelia Turner. I confess that I find it hard to renounce my first impression.
[42] *Stanzas. — April, 1814*, 21–24.

162   POWER AND ELUSIVENESS IN SHELLEY

The same poem, which comprises only twenty-four lines, contains another mention of smiles, "midnight's frown and morning's smile."[43] "An infant's smile" is the simile applied to the flowers in the close of the forty-ninth stanza of *Adonais*.

The smile figures among the most august companionships. The smiles of Asia before they dwindle make the cold air fire;[44] the great Prometheus is arrayed in smiles;[45] the universal spirit is "That Light whose smile kindles the Universe."[46] Not only pathos, as in *Rosalind and Helen*, but terror, as in *The Cenci*, may be expressed in smiles. Lucretia asks:

> Could it be worse
> Than when he smiled, and cried, My sons are dead![47]

It is the smile of Cenci that chills Beatrice to the heart:

> It was one word, Mother, one little word;
> One look, one smile [48]

Cenci himself is aware of its malign efficacy. In one of the most appalling passages in the drama, he says:

> A man you knew spoke of my wife and daughter —
> He was accustomed to frequent my house;
> So the next day *his* wife and daughter came
> And asked if I had seen him; and I smiled:
> I think they never saw him any more [49]

III. Irradiation. The word "irradiation," which is rather a makeshift than an adequate tool, is here used to signify something emanating from an object which

---

[43] *Ibid.*, 16.   [44] *Prometheus Unbound*, II. v. 50–51.   [45] *Ibid.*, II. i. 120–21.
[46] *Adonais*, liv. 1.   [47] *The Cenci*, II. i. 36–37.   [48] *Ibid.*, II. i. 63–64.
[49] *Ibid.*, I. i. 61–65.

EFFLUENCE

thereafter stands to that object in the relation of an envelope, an atmosphere, or an aureole. Shelley is particularly fond of this process and of this relation. In many cases it is light which the object supplies to make itself visible or to guide its conduct:

> vials which shone
> In their own golden beams [50]

> So came a chariot on the silent storm
> Of its own rushing splendour [51]

> And saw by the warm light of their own life
> Her glowing limbs beneath the sinuous veil
> Of woven wind,[52]

> An eagle alit one moment may sit
> In the light of its golden wings [53]

> And pleasure, blind with tears, led by the gleam
> Of her own dying smile instead of eyes [54]

The utility of light in the absence of eyesight is a point left to the reader's imagination or his charity.

> 'tis He, arrayed
> In the soft light of his own smiles,[55]

> The Spirit of the Earth is laid asleep,
> And you can see its little lips are moving,
> Amid the changing light of their own smiles,[56]

Shelley has a remarkable way of conceiving beauty as a highly rarefied but physical emanation hanging around or suffusing the object from which it springs

---

[50] *The Witch of Atlas*, xx. 5–6.
[51] *The Triumph of Life*, 86–87.
[52] *Alastor*, 175–77.   [53] *The Cloud*, 37–38.   [54] *Adonais*. xiii. 6–7.
[55] *Prometheus Unbound*, II. i. 120–21.   [56] *Ibid.*, IV. 265–67.

like an aerial vestment or a lucid atmosphere. It is as if in the first place he separated — in both the literal and figurative senses of the word, abstracted — the beauty from the object, and then proceeded to reincorporate this abstraction in the shape of a subtile atmosphere or nimbus — aura or corona — embosoming and embellishing the object. This is very fantastic, but that is no argument against its occurrence in the mystical and daring mind of Shelley. Emerson quotes Proclus as affirming of beauty that it "swims on the light of forms." Another analogy, though a faint one, to Shelley's conception of the matter is found in the line of Coleridge in reference to Christabel:

> Her gentle limbs did she undress
> And lay down in her loveliness [57]

Here it is almost impossible not to regard the loveliness as, in a sort, the substitute for the garments which have been laid aside, and the conception has some analogy with that of Shelley in the following passages:

> As a youth lulled in love-dreams faintly sighing,
> Under the shadow of his beauty lying,
> Which round his rest a watch of light and warmth doth keep.[58]

Here the youth lies in the *shadow* of his own beauty, and this shadow or this beauty which is a shadow keeps a watch of *light* around his rest. I point out this fact, not in the way of cavil, but merely to show that a flat contradiction between two images is no bar to their

[57] *Christabel*, i. 237–38. [58] *Prometheus Unbound*, IV. 447–49.

simultaneous harborage in the uncritical mind of Shelley. The boldness of the metaphor in the watch of light and warmth is almost without parallel even in the poet himself; but his success is the justification of his rashness. A passage not so bold but perhaps even more beautiful is found in *The Witch of Atlas.*

>   as she lay unfolden
> In the warm shadow of her loveliness [59]

Again in the same poem,

>   they
> Move in the light of their own beauty thus [60]

The subject in the following is a snake:

> When he floats on that dark and lucid flood
> In the light of his own loveliness [61]

In the following a plant is the subject:

> And thus it lay in the Elysian calm
> Of its own beauty [62]

> Thou art folded, thou art lying
> In the light which is undying
> Of thine own joy, and heaven's smile divine; [63]

Here are four passages of a slightly different character:

> others mournfully within the gloom
> Of their own shadow walked and called it death [64]

> Others, with burning eyes, lean forth, and drink
> With eager lips the wind of their own speed, [65]

---

[59] *The Witch of Atlas,* ii. 4–5.   [60] *Ibid.,* lxv. 5–6.
[61] *Rosalind and Helen,* 118–19. [62] *Fragments of an Unfinished Drama,* 228–29.
[63] *Prometheus Unbound,* IV. 437–39.   [64] *The Triumph of Life,* 58–59.
[65] *Prometheus Unbound,* II. iv. 135–36.

> In deeds which make the Christian cause look pale
> In its own light [66]
>
> In thoughts and joys which sleep, but cannot die,
> Folded within their own eternity [67]

The conception of eternity, in the first place, as an attribute of particular thoughts and joys and, in the second place, as an envelope or investiture in which they are folded should be compared with the thought, that is, the murderous design, of Beatrice:

> like a ghost shrouded and folded up
> In its own formless horror [68]

The use of the word "own," his own, her own, its own, their own, is characteristic of Shelley, and is an index of his fondness for the detection of relations between objects and their own effluxes or offspring. It is surprising that the procession of the Holy Ghost did not tempt him to the acceptance of the doctrine of the Trinity.

IV. Personality. The influence of one personality upon another may be, according to Shelley's view, great, penetrative, and mysterious. Examples have already been given of the permeation of one spirit by another, of the absorption of soul by soul, of the mystic union or identification of two beings. To some of these we may recur, but we will begin with fresh examples:

> He paused, and to my lips he bent
> His own: like spirit his words went
> Through all my limbs with the speed of fire;

---

[66] *Hellas*, 554–55.   [67] *Epipsychidion*, 523–24.   [68] *The Cenci*, III. i. 110–11.

> And his keen eyes, glittering through mine,
> Filled me with the flame divine,
> Which in their orbs was burning far,[69]

The effect of this magnetization is to endow Helen with a musical skill unknown to her normal experience.

> Yet look on me — take not thine eyes away,
> Which feed upon the love within mine own,
> Which is indeed but the reflected ray
> Of thine own beauty from my spirit thrown.[70]

The complexity of this must not be overlooked. The beauty of one spirit is reflected in the love of the other, and this love is fed upon by the eyes of the first. As an instance of the Shelleyan subtlety, observe the following:

> The beauty of delight makes lovers glad
> Gazing on one another [71]

Most of us would have said the delight of beauty, but the beauty is subtly conceived to be the effect or manifestation of the delight.

In *The Sensitive Plant* the Lady is the soul of the garden; its beauty is an irradiation from her spirit and vanishes at her death. The same idea is expressed in a different form in *To Jane: The Recollection*. The beauty of the external scene is described, but its source is felt to be apart from itself, to be but an emanation from the form of Jane.

> And still I felt the centre of
> The magic circle there

---

[69] *Rosalind and Helen*, 1131–36. [70] *To——*, "Yet look not on me," 1–4.
[71] *Prometheus Unbound*, I. 465–66.

> Was one fair form that filled with love
> The lifeless atmosphere.[72]

To conceive the beauty of the outward universe as a reflection or emanation of the divine love is quite natural and fitting, since the universe may properly express the feelings of its author; but to attribute this beauty to the effect of a human presence which is not the author of the external world is a step too bold and too mystical not to find welcome in the mind of Shelley. The Indian vale in which Asia dwells was once frozen and desolate, but her presence has operated like spring in the evocation of flowers, herbs, sweet airs, and sounds.[73]

>   the light
> Which fills this vapor, as the aëreal hue
> Of fountain-gazing roses fills the water,
> Flows from thy mighty sister.[74]

The poet's sensitiveness to effluence is as clearly shown in the simile, the reddening of water by the roses that border it, as in the primary thought. A very similar image, also illustrative of a moral truth, is found in the first act.

> As from the rose which the pale priestess kneels
> To gather for her festal crown of flowers
> The aerial crimson falls, flushing her cheek,
> So from our victim's destined agony
> The shade which is our form invests us round;
> Else we are shapeless as our mother Night.[75]

[72] Lines 49–52.
[73] *Prometheus Unbound*, I. 826–33.
[74] *Ibid.*, II. v. 11–14.
[75] *Ibid.*, I. 467–72.

Here the agony — and not the present but the foreseen or future agony — of one being is said to exhale the form which invests another, its tormentor. The psychology of mysticism can hardly go further.

To return to Asia: love bursts from her, and illumines earth, heaven, ocean, the sunless caves, and all who dwell within them.[76] The relations between Prometheus, Asia, Panthea, and Ione are sufficiently occult and complex: Asia never sleeps but when the shadow of the spirit of Prometheus falls upon her.[77] But as Asia is far from Prometheus, this shadow has to be carried by Panthea, who is addressed by Asia as the beloved and beautiful one

> who wearest
> The shadow of that soul by which I live.[78]

The spirit of Prometheus transfuses itself into that of Panthea while she sleeps; his nature saturates and absorbs hers; and his message to Asia is visible in her eyes when she seeks her sister at dawn in the Indian Caucasus. But Ione has been sleeping in Panthea's embrace, and a life and warmth, not her own, but transmitted, it would seem, from Prometheus through Panthea, has permeated her body.

The stellar and planetary emanations in the fourth act are well worth noting, but I must confine myself to one quotation:

> Thou art folded, thou art lying
> In the light which is undying

---

[76] *Ibid.*, II. v. 26–30.　　[77] *Ibid.*, I. 822–23.　　[78] *Ibid.*, II. i. 30–31.

> Of thine own joy, and heaven's smile divine;
> All suns and constellations shower
> On thee a light, a life, a power
> Which doth array thy sphere; thou pourest thine
> On mine, on mine! [79]

Shelley seems to have been rather less interested in magnetism and mesmerism than might have been expected from his great, not to say exaggerated, estimate of the effect of one personality upon another. He permitted Medwin to try the effect of mesmerism on his irritable nerves with results which were eminently satisfactory, at least to the operator. Subsequent experiments on the part of a lady (Mrs. Williams) led to the composition of a poem entitled *The Magnetic Lady to Her Patient,* which throws less light on Shelley's views of magnetism and effluence than on the more normal relation between himself and the practitioner. I suspect the truth to be that the habitual — it could scarcely be called the ordinary — effect of other persons on Shelley was so strong that the addition of any occult power was undesired and uncalled-for. A man who could say of himself, "I pant, I sink, I tremble, I expire" [80] under the influence of mere love or friendship might well find something adventitious and redundant in the use of magnetic or mesmeric agencies.

[79] *Ibid.,* IV. 437–43; see also IV. 325–31, 356–59, 450–56.
[80] *Epipsychidion,* 591.

Pantheism

THE SUBJECT of effluence leads naturally to that of pantheism, at least to that form of pantheism in which all aspects of mind and matter are regarded as emanations or irradiations from a single divine source. Pantheism in this form unites the two qualities of power and mystery, of impressiveness and intangibility, in a degree unknown or at least uncongenial to any other theory. Atheism gives rise to some difficult questions; but in itself it is a plain, straight-edged, well-defined conception — the conception, in short, of those to whom mystery and elusiveness are displeasing. Theism also has its troublesome problems, but the notions of an architect of the universe or of a father of mankind are, if taken by themselves and not too closely compared with facts, perfectly definite and substantial notions. Neither of these ideas provokes and baffles the imagination to anything like the same extent to which it perplexes the reason. But pantheism is the conception which allures and evades, which tempts the mind of the dreamer and poet to follow it into those dim recesses in which it escapes at last from the ardor of pursuit. It follows that pantheism, in the sense of a supreme universal force of which all objects were the products and the representations, was Shelley's theory of the universe.

The documents, if I may call them so, which unfold this theory are: (1) the Necessity passage in *Queen*

Mab[1] with the accompanying prose note; (2) the opening of *Alastor;*[2] (3) *Mont Blanc;* (4) the passage in the *Lines written among the Euganean Hills;*[3] (5) the *Hymn to Intellectual Beauty;* (6) the fourth fragment in *Prince Athanase;*[4] (7) the responses of Demogorgon to Asia;[5] (8) the conclusion of *Adonais;*[6] and (9) the last epode in the *Ode to Naples.*[7]

In the *Queen Mab* passage Shelley invokes the universal force under the abstract and lifeless name of "Necessity." It is "a spirit of activity and life," "eternal," inflexible in its course, devoid of will and of morality, operative equally and impartially in the "fair oak" and "the poison-tree," in the "good man" and

> the slave
> Whose horrible lusts spread misery o'er the world.[8]

We have here the doctrine of Necessity in its most rigorous and pitiless and also, it must be confessed, its least suggestive and least poetical form. There are traces, however, even in this passage of a revolt or protest of the young poet's imagination against the rigors of his high-handed logic. The noble adjective "steadfast"[9] is applied to this unmoral force; it is designated not only as "Spirit of Nature"[10] but as "Soul of the Universe";[11] it is even addressed in the tenderest of conceivable appellations as "Necessity! thou mother of the world!"[12] a term which may be taken, if one pleases, merely in

---

[1] vi. 146–238.   [2] Lines 1–49.   [3] Lines 285–319.
[4] iv. 1–19.   [5] *Prometheus Unbound*, II. iv. *passim.*   [6] Stanzas lii–lv.
[7] Lines 149–76.   [8] *Queen Mab*, vi. 203–04.   [9] *Ibid.*, vi. 156.
[10] *Ibid.*, vi. 197.   [11] *Ibid.*, ii. 190.   [12] *Ibid.*, vi. 198.

the sense of originator, but which is nevertheless interesting in view of Shelley's repudiation at this time of the doctrine of the fatherhood of God and of the subsequent adoption of this very term of "mother" by Unitarian theologians in the effort to make God even more tenderly and humanly sympathetic than He appeared in His paternal character.

In *Alastor* less than three years later there is clear proof of a radical change. The barren and lifeless "Necessity" is replaced by a spirit capable of being loved, a spirit whom Shelley has loved from the first, and on whom he heaps the most august and hallowed titles that affection tempered by reverence could suggest. This spirit is "our great Mother," the "Mother of this unfathomable world," and the "Great Parent."[13] It is associated with the feelings for landscape, even with landscape itself: earth, ocean, and air are a beloved brotherhood, the offspring with Shelley himself of the universal parent.[14] He has sought intercourse with this power by visits to charnels and coffins in the hope of surprising some communicative ghost.[15] He has sought revelations in another way, the account of which may be best given in his own words:

> Have I mixed awful talk and asking looks
> With my most innocent love, until strange tears
> Uniting with those breathless kisses, made
> Such magic as compels the charmèd night
> To render up thy charge:[16]

[13] *Alastor*, 2, 18, 45. [14] *Ibid.*, 1–2.
[15] *Ibid.*, 23–29. [16] *Ibid.*, 33–37.

This appears to refer to the bodily conjunction of the sexes, and is a further proof of the typical or imaginative nature of Shelley's interest in that form of pleasure. These efforts seem to have in great measure failed, since the real sources of such partial knowledge as has been vouchsafed to him are affirmed later to have been "incommunicable dream, and twilight phantasms, and deep noonday thought."[17] One of the most remarkable things about the passage is its deeply and unfeignedly reverential tone. The doctrine of Necessity in *Queen Mab* is clearly felt to be a thesis or theorem and is sustained as such. The revolution apparent in *Alastor* is startling; but the new faith is not defended; it is scarcely even asserted: it is assumed. The whole passage might be taken by a mind unacquainted with Shelley to be the index of a long-established and deep-seated piety — a faith reaching back without interruption to the cradle.

Reverence solemnizing love and love softening reverence give the keynote to the solemn apostrophe with which *Alastor* opens. In *Mont Blanc,* where the setting and occasion are found among the most austere and awful of natural forms, reverence is the only sentiment and rises to an awe not unmixed with oppression and terror. It is a severe, a somber, almost a savage power, which enlarges and quiets, even while in a fashion it shadows and burdens, the mind.

> The wilderness has a mysterious tongue
> Which teaches awful doubt, or faith so mild,

[17] *Ibid.,* 39–40.

PANTHEISM

So solemn, so serene, that man may be
But for such faith with Nature reconciled; [18]

Power dwells apart in its tranquillity
Remote, serene, and inaccessible.[19]

> The secret strength of things,
> Which governs thought, and to the infinite dome
> Of heaven is as a law, inhabits thee! [20]

Mont Blanc in relation to *Alastor* is a proof of the plasticity of the idea of deity in Shelley's mind; it varied with surroundings and mood.

The *Hymn to Intellectual Beauty* is very like the opening passage of *Alastor* in the solemnity of its tone, in the renewed mention of the search for ghosts, and even in the repeated allusion to the bodily satisfactions of love, implied in the phrase "love's delight." [21] The revelations of the great spirit are still affirmed, but their evanescence is dwelt upon with pathetic repetition. Beauty, which has scarcely been named in the preceding passages, is now the dominant note, but it is beauty imbued with awe — an "awful shadow," [22] an "awful Loveliness." [23] The direct reference to the higher love is confined to the last line, where the spirit has bound the poet to fear himself and love all humankind.[24] It is in this poem that the first express identification of this great power with the spirit of liberty is to be noticed:

> never joy illumed my brow
> Unlinked with hope that thou wouldst free
> This world from its dark slavery,[25]

[18] *Mont Blanc*, 76-79. [19] *Ibid.*, 96-97. [20] *Ibid.*, 139-41. [21] vi. 6.
[22] i. 1. [23] vi. 11. [24] vii. 7. [25] vi. 8-10.

In this, perhaps the most complete and perfect of all Shelley's expositions of his mature faith, the mixture of charm and elusiveness is especially noticeable. No faith could be more exquisite, none perhaps more evasive, than that which is portrayed in the noble *Hymn* and the stately invocation in *Alastor*.

The passage in the *Euganean Hills* is chiefly interesting for the close neighborhood and fellowship established between material and immaterial things as the common tenements or conductors of the great spirit. In such a passage as

> Be it love, light, harmony,
> Odour, or the soul of all [26]

the poet passes as readily from love to light as another man would from light to sound, and as easily from "odour" to the "soul of all" as another might from thought to feeling.

The fourth fragment of *Prince Athanase* is another hymn to love, opening with a sort of Bacchic transport:

> Thou art the wine whose drunkenness is all
> We can desire, O Love [27]

The orgiastic note of this opening, which prepares for something like that which Mr. Swinburne afterwards executed in *Dolores,* the lady of Pain, is not kept at its first pitch, or even kept at all, through the remainder of the short fragment. The chaster pantheistic creed reappears in the representation of the spirit under the universal and pervasive forms of light and air; its

[26] Lines 315–16.   [27] vi. 1–2.

PANTHEISM

shadow lets fall beauty upon the landscape, and floats among souls with its solicitations to gentleness and goodness.

The fourth scene of the second act of *Prometheus Unbound* is unique among Shelley's confessions of faith for the adoption of the form of a catechism and for the striking but untrustworthy note of orthodoxy which in the first passage dominates both the thoughts and the language.

> *Asia.*   Who made all
> That it contains? thought, passion, reason, will
> Imagination?
> *Demogorgon.* God: Almighty God.[28]

At first sight it seems as if Shelley's spirit of religious revolt, commonly directed against the ideas of his contemporaries, was turned for a moment against his own, as if the great rebel had sought variety in insurrection by becoming for the time being a rebel to himself. The use of the term "God," the application of the word "made" to the world or universe, are utterly foreign to the poet's habits. The next question is more Shelleyan: Asia wishes to know the source of the mysterious and delightful feelings which are evoked in our hearts by the passage of the winds of spring, or the voice of one who is dear to us. Demogorgon's answer, however, is still thoroughly orthodox: "Merciful God," [29] he replies. All this, however, is virtually recanted later on. After some discourse on Saturn, Jupiter, and Prome-

[28] *Prometheus Unbound*, II. iv. 9–11.
[29] *Ibid.*, II. iv. 18.

theus, Asia wishes to know if Jove is a slave, and, if so, who is his master? The dialogue continues thus:

> *Demogorgon.* All spirits are enslaved which serve things evil:
> Thou knowest if Jupiter be such or no.
> *Asia.* Whom calledst thou God?
> *Demogorgon.* I spoke but as ye speak,
> For Jove is the supreme of living things.
> *Asia.* Who is the master of the slave?
> *Demogorgon.* If the abysm
> Could vomit forth its secrets — but a voice
> Is wanting, the deep truth is imageless;
> For what would it avail to bid thee gaze
> On the revolving world? What to bid speak
> Fate, Time, Occasion, Chance and Change? To these
> All things are subject but eternal Love.[30]

Asia's speech, "Whom calledst thou God?" seems to mean: "Why do you not tell me who is Jupiter's master? Is it not the God of whom you were just speaking?" To which Demogorgon replies in effect: "In calling this power God I merely fell in with conventional usage. He is not God nor master; these human and personal terms do not apply to him. Of all living, that is, of all organic, human, or human-like beings Jupiter is the chief." In the next reply he indicates vaguely the nature of the controlling forces. Jove is subject to the abstract powers, "Fate, Time, Occasion, Chance and Change,"[31] and these in turn are subject to the greater abstraction, "Eternal Love." This is the true Shelleyan faith to which we have returned by a circuit that had

[30] *Ibid.*, II. iv. 110-20.   [31] *Ibid.*, II. iv. 119.

its starting-point in the apparent contradiction of these principles. The interpretation above given is the one which seems to me to accord best with reason and the context, but the passage is too vague and too elliptical to permit an incontestable exegesis.

In *Adonais* the solemn vein of mingled awfulness and beauty is once more in the ascendant. The relation between the spirit and its manifestations is more clearly marked than ever before in the famous

> Life like a dome of many-coloured glass
> Stains the white radiance of Eternity [32]

and the "white radiance" involves a degree of pure abstraction and isolation which Shelley has scarce given elsewhere to his conception of deity. Later on the ideas of beauty and love are again emphasized and the unequal or graduated participation of all things and creatures in the divine essence is brought out with distinctness.

The last but not least interesting of the testimonies is found in the *Ode to Naples*. The central power in this indignant and martial ode is invoked under what might seem the anomalous title of "Great Spirit, deepest Love!" [33] and this moral essence is treated like a physical force in the directness and thoroughness of its control over matter.

> Which rulest and dost move
> All things which live and are, within the Italian shore;
> Who spreadest heaven around it,
> Whose woods, rocks, waves, surround it; [34]

[32] lii. 3–4.   [33] *Ode to Naples*, 149.   [34] *Ibid.*, 150–53.

So complete is its mastery of this instrument that it is even asked to utilize the sunbeams and the showers in the destruction — so opposed to the conventional idea of love — of the invaders and tyrants of Naples.[35] By another curious contrast this "Love," so lofty and martial and vindictive, is associated by a double allusion with the type of sensuous, self-indulgent, and earthly love, the planet Venus.[36] We have here another proof of the smallness of the gap between the bodily and the spiritual passion in Shelley's mind, correspondent with the narrowness of the chasm dividing mind from matter. What is even more significant is the complete and express identification of this love and beauty with the great cause of Neapolitan, and (by implication) universal freedom — a fusion of which we had but a scant hint in the *Hymn to Intellectual Beauty*. Thus the great trinity is complete: the delight in nature, the thirst for love, the aspiration toward freedom, the three great mainsprings, perhaps, of the poet's life and verse, combine and center in the worship of the great power of which beauty, love, and freedom are distinct but not discrepant manifestations. The god of Shelley is a powerful, enthralling, mystical, and elusive force, the fit complement of his desires and temper.

[35] *Ibid.*, 155–64.   [36] *Ibid.*, 154, 167.

Metaphysics

I PROPOSE to refer in this place to some of the metaphysical doctrines held by Shelley which illustrate his fondness for the intangible and powerful.

1. The belief in the immortality of the soul. Shelley's acceptance of this view is supported by many passages, but the subject is weighty enough to demand an essay to itself and I content myself here by referring the reader to the *Adonais* passage [1] and the pictures of the next world in the first and twelfth cantos of *The Revolt of Islam*.[2]

2. The belief in progressive states of the same individual implied in the following:

The first stanza contrasts the immortality of the living and thinking beings which inhabit the planets, and to use a common and inadequate phrase, *clothe themselves in matter*, with the transience of the noblest manifestations of the external world.

The concluding verses indicate a progressive state of more or less exalted existence, according to the degree of perfection which every distinct intelligence may have attained.[3]

Shelley cannot be said, however, to have laid stress on this idea.

3. The belief in the everlastingness of beautiful things, their seeming death being the consequence of the imperfection of our organs.

---

[1] Stanzas xxxix–xlvi.   [2] I. xlix–lx; XII. xxxii–xli.
[3] Note 2 to *Hellas* (Chorus, i. 197 *et seq.*).

> That garden sweet, that lady fair,
> And all sweet shapes and odours there,
> In truth have never passed away:
> 'Tis we, 'tis ours, are changed; not they.
>
> For love, and beauty, and delight,
> There is no death nor change: their might
> Exceeds our organs, which endure
> No light, being themselves obscure.[4]

4. The belief in the unreality of matter. This is emphatically stated in *Queen Mab*: "Soul is the only element."[5] Compare the following from *Epipsychidion*:

> the Earth and Ocean seem
> To sleep in one another's arms, and dream
> Of waves, flowers, clouds, woods, rocks, and all that we
> Read in their smiles, and call reality.[6]

5. The conception of life as an unreality, a phantasm, the veil of a more real world.

> Life's phantasmal scene [7]

> this phantasmal scene [8]

> this familiar life, which seems to be
> But is not [9]

> Death is the veil which those who live call life:
> They sleep and it is lifted: [10]

> The painted veil, by those who were, called life,
> Which mimicked, as with colours idly spread,
> All men believed and hoped, is torn aside; [11]

---

[4] *The Sensitive Plant*, Conclusion, 17–24.
[5] iv. 140.
[6] Lines 509–12.
[7] *Queen Mab*, ix. 74.
[8] *Alastor*, 697.
[9] *Letter to Maria Gisborne*, 156–57.
[10] *Prometheus Unbound*, III. iii. 113–14.
[11] *Ibid.*, III. iv. 190–92.

METAPHYSICS

>Lift not the painted veil which those who live
>Call Life; though unreal shapes be pictured there,
>And it but mimic all we would believe
>With colours idly spread,[12]
>
>>in this life
>
>. . . . .
>Where nothing is, but all things seem,
>And we the shadows of the dream [13]

6. The belief in the unreality of Time and Space. The first quotation is from *Hellas,* a poem singular for its union of metaphysical depth with romantic splendor:

>The future and the past are idle shadows
>Of thought's eternal flight — they have no being [14]

A poet participates in the eternal, the infinite, and the one; as far as relates to his conceptions, time and place and number are not.[15]

7. The conception of art expressed in the following passage:

>>lovely apparitions, dim at first,
>Then radiant, as the mind, arising bright
>From the embrace of beauty, whence the forms
>Of which these are the phantoms, casts on them
>The gathered rays which are reality,
>Shall visit us, the progeny immortal
>Of Painting, Sculpture, and rapt Poesy,
>And arts, though unimagined, yet to be.[16]

I take this to mean that as beauty produces the forms of the outward world so the mind, fertilized by com-

---
[12] *Sonnet, 1818,* 1-4.   [13] *The Sensitive Plant,* Conclusion, 9-12.
[14] Lines 783-84.   [15] *A Defence of Poetry,* p. 104.
[16] *Prometheus Unbound,* III. iii. 49-56.

munion with this beauty, produces the artistic works which are the images or phantoms of the works of nature, and that the matter used in this process, originally phantasmal and unsubstantial like all matter, becomes real only by impregnation from the source of reality, the mind. Those who wish to appreciate the mystical element in Shelley's conception of art should read *A Defence of Poetry,* an essay which is penetrated by this subtile property in a form better suited to be felt as a whole than to take shape in defined and separable quotations.

Summary

THE EVIDENCE in support of my thesis is now complete. In the effort to prove that Shelley was characterized to an unusual degree by a passion for objects which united the qualities of power and elusiveness, of momentousness and intangibility, I cited in the first place his well-known predilection for the abstract. I next showed that he was especially impressed by the most abstract of all abstractions, Space and Time, and that his feeling for Time, in particular, was of a sort not readily to be matched in literature. His feeling for mind as mind was then taken up, and it was shown that he shared to the full in the ordinary poetic habit of illustrating psychic facts by physical images; that in addition to this he displayed the rather unusual habit of illustrating physical facts by psychic images; and that last of all he was characterized by a third habit — almost peculiar to himself — of effacing or all but effacing the boundary between the opposed worlds of mind and matter. I then showed by testimony that his interest in sleep, in dreams, and in ghosts, three objects remarkable for the combination of power and elusiveness, was extraordinarily vivid. I passed next to a discussion of landscape. It was shown that wind and cloud, two of the least tangible substances in nature, were the objects of a peculiar and passionate attachment. Light, sound, and odor, three of the most affecting yet also three of the least definite of physical manifestations, were found to be conspicuous among the objects of his unstinted and unchanging affection. That his conception of these objects was in a high degree abstract was proved by his constant use of the abstract terms, by his habit of linking the ideas together, by his fashion of illustrating each by images derived from the others, and even of directly affirming their mutual conversion or transformation. I next showed the keenness of Shelley's interest in the occult but attractive processes of penetration, solution, absorption, and the like. Effluence was then taken up and the exceptional nature of Shelley's interest in shadows, in smiles, in the aura or atmosphere exhaled from a personality, in the mysterious and magnetic effects of one soul upon another was shown by forcible examples. I took up next the subject of pantheism, and analyzed the form assumed in the mind of Shelley by this most fascinating and at the same time most impalpable of faiths. Last of all a number of Shelley's metaphysical tenets supporting the general thesis were adduced.

My readers must form their own judgment of the worth of this evidence; my own study of the subject has left me with a feeling of surprise at its strength and its variety. The proposition, as stated at the outset, would probably be conceded off-hand by most competent critics; but unless I deceive myself, the thesis itself has grown in magnitude and moment with each new increment to the accumulating proofs. Everyone would grant at the start that the union of the two qualities is characteristic of Shelley's verse in a considerable degree. I have aimed to show, and I trust that I have shown, that his verse is characterized by this union in an extraordinary, I might almost say in an unprecedented, degree. For my own part, I am far from regarding these proofs solely in the light of their ability to sustain a thesis; I have valued the proposition almost as much for the sake of the evidence as the evidence for the sake of the proposition. There is a wide difference between equally gifted writers in the number of interesting things that can be ascertained and reported of them; and the number of interesting things to be said of Shelley's works as of his life is surprisingly great. He was a man of many literary habits, and a man who pushed nearly every habit to an extreme; he is therefore peculiarly fitted to recompense the faithful investigator. That the present effort may not be quite barren of result in the elucidation of one of the most gifted and lovable of human spirits is the hope in which I close this essay.